Praise for C___

'Success in business is about releasing potential – Colin's definitive work does just that' Ken Moran, Chairman, Pfizer Limited

'Highly researched yet intuitive' Neil Holloway, General Manager, Microsoft Limited

'Where others promise, Colin delivers' Adrian Hosford, Director TalkWorks, British Telecom.

'Highly recommended' *Financial Times*

'East meets West for successful business' His Excellency, Ma Zengang, Chinese Ambassador

'Powerfully provokes your thinking' Steve Parrish, Director IBM

'Powerful, practical ideas; simple yet so effective' Investors in People

'Colin's philosophy works' Chris Cowdray, General Manager, Claridge's Savoy Group

'Compulsory reading' Dr Marilyn Orcharton, Founder of Denplan

'Thought provoking' Young Presidents Organisation

'What Colin has to share is worth reading' *Business Age*

'I sincerely hope millions read Colin's work' Sir Michael Grylls, Former Chairman of the Small Business Bureau

'Straight to the point!' Benny Higgins, Managing Director, Retail Banking, The Royal Bank of Scotland plc

'Colin's been there and knows what he is talking about' *Success Today*

'Your work is a powerful conduit for success' Sir Douglas Morpeth, Former Chairman Clerical Medical.

'You cannot afford not to know what this man is teaching' Richard Denny, Author of *Selling to Win*

'A commonsense and principled approach that brings lasting results' George McWatters, Founder of HTV

'What Turner preaches he has practised, out there' *Sunday Independent*

'In the 21st Century competitive advantage will be based on corporate creativity. In a challenging and insightful manner this excellent book brings together the individual and organisational qualities needed for companies to achieve this' Professor Richard Scase

Shooting the Monkey

Monkey

Secrets of the New Business Spirit

Colin Turner

CORONET BOOKS
Hodder and Stoughton

First published in Great Britain in 1999 by Hodder and Stoughton
First published in paperback in 2000 by Hodder and Stoughton
A division of Hodder Headline

A Coronet Paperback

10 9 8 7 6 5 4 3 2 1

A CIP record for this book is available
from the British Library

ISBN 0 340 72891 4

Printed and bound in Great Britain by
Mackays of Chatham plc, Chatham, Kent

Hodder and Stoughton
A division of Hodder Headline
338 Euston Road
London NW1 3BH

Dedicated to Wei Tzu

To Adnan,

Thanks for.

reviewing The Dome!

Warmest Wishes

John

26/01/00

Acknowledgements

My greatest gift is my family. I believe that it is impossible to devote one's self to writing a book without the devotion of others. I thank my family for their love; it inspired me when I lacked inspiration. And I thank my wife, whose consistent belief, confidence, tolerance and support in both me and my work remains a very special source of strength.

A particular thank you to my publishers, Hodder & Stoughton, for their continued deliverance in spreading this philosophy. Special thanks to my editor, Rowena Webb, and to Laura Brockbank. Also to Mark Reynolds, Diana Riley, Camilla Sweeney, Briar Silich and Sheila Crowley.

To my friends, clients and the countless people I have met at seminars and diverse organisations from around the world — thank you for giving me the opportunity to share with, and learn from, you all.

Thanks to the literary mentors and philosophers, both present and past, who have influenced my thinking. Particular gratitude to Chang Tzu, Hazrat Khan, Master Ni Hou Ching, Vernon Howard, Paul Brunton, Alan Cohen, Wayne Dyer, Sheik Muzaffer, Emerson, Rumi, Lao Tzu, George Gurdjieff, Sri Swami Satchidananda and God.

CONTENTS

Unlocking the Secrets of the New Business Spirit

There is a legend that tells of a famous Academy, now lost in the mountains of an Eastern Province. Founded some two-and-a-half millennia ago by an immensely successful Patriarch, Wei Tzu, the School attracted the interest of great leaders and merchants, all earnestly seeking the secrets of a new business alchemy.

Possibly a member of the inner circle of Taoist sages, Wei Tzu would have been fully versed in the metaphysical secrets of the ancients. His paradoxical philosophy, therefore, would almost certainly have followed the way of self-mastery through individual inner understanding.

Over several generations the School's acclaim grew, through word of mouth, as each student, enlightened by their understanding of this new business spirit, graduated. However, in the year 213BC almost all remnants of this ancient teaching were destroyed by the first Emperor of what we now consider to be geographical China, the ruthless Ch'in Shih Huang-ti. He was convinced that if all such wisdom was destroyed, no-one would understand that life could be any different from that under his dictatorship. No-one could question or usurp him.

Pursuing this policy to control society's thinking, his brutal Prime Minister, Li Ssu, ordered countless sages, merchants and scholars to be executed and their places of learning and trading to be burned to the ground. In an attempt to save them from destruction, valuable scrolls and texts were hidden in hollowed walls, a time-honoured custom utilised by numerous cultures over the ages.

As for Emperor Ch'in, history records that his empire lasted only during his lifetime, a mere forty-one years. A vivid reminder that strategies founded on manipulation and control are always short-lived. Unwittingly, he had destroyed the wisdom that could have been his greatest strength as a leader.

We currently live in an age where, despite continuous improvement and the immense power at our fingertips, the majority of businesses still last less than a generation, and most people retire with little money. Clearly, the application of a new business spirit is as vitally important and valid today as it was to leaders and achievers over two millennia ago.

Certainly the Western world, albeit imperceptibly, is gradually moving away from mindless consumption, preferring sustainable quality over disposable quantity. Increasingly, businesses are seeking strategic alliances with competitors in order to develop the co-operation essential to serve mutual customers. People are becoming more aware that the labels of *me*, *my* and *mine* impose artificial limitations on their enjoyment of life, recognising that the key is to think *we*, *us* and *ours*. Enlightenment will inevitably replace the emptiness offered by empowerment, as people become increasingly conscious that being true to why they are, and how they feel about what they do for others, is more important than concern over who they are, and what they can solicit from others.

Inevitably, there are many delusions to be cleared, but without doubt there is an increasing wave of consciousness that embraces the understanding of our own universality, and accepts the responsibility to move from egotistical separation towards such 'oneness'. Those who become enlightened will be the leaders and achievers of the modern world without struggle.

Effort will be required, but only those who cling to what they know will continue to struggle. The future is not what it used to be, and nor can it *be* so, because of the very dynamics that are driving the wave.

The thought-provoking lessons taught by forgotten sages and harnessed by great leaders and merchants are revealed within this book. Paradoxically, through their initial obscurity they clearly provide the answers currently sought by our modern business world. Although these two-thousand-year-old revelations shake the pillars of traditional business thinking, they uncannily strike chords within us, because of the sound truths that resonate from them. That is because achieving self-mastery through individual inner understanding is the only sure and timeless way to fully develop our potential, achieve our purpose and ensure our spiritual growth.

Work can no longer be viewed as a separate compartment to the way we live our lives, both personally and professionally. There is an emerging demand for meaningful, purposeful and sustainable success, and as a business intuitive seeking to provide the philosophies essential for this demand, my own research and practical studies led to me writing this book. In doing so, I sought to unlock and share esoteric secrets and explain forgotten alchemy in the form of twelve scrolls. They encapsulate, through metaphorical parables, my interpretation of the genre of ancient wisdom, as possibly taught in Wei Tzu's Business Academy.

It is my sincere belief that by reading *Shooting the Monkey*, the opportunity to test the potency of its ideas will immediately present itself. In this way, I know that you, my reader, will become your own graduate of self-mastery and a true alchemist of the new business spirit.

Colin Turner
Upper Littleton, Somerset
England

The First Scroll: Riding the Tiger

The Secret of Channelling Your Energy Correctly

'Today my eldest son, Ni, joins us,' said Merchant Hui Neng proudly, to all the agents and workers gathered together. 'Ni has studied under many teachers who assure me that he will prove to be our most valuable asset.'

Having built up his business from nothing, Hui Neng had been determined that his eldest son would not be deprived of a good all-round education. For Ni's part there had been many lessons. He had excelled at rhetoric and debate, which he'd really enjoyed, and was able to express himself eloquently. But he had done so badly at his figure work that his tutors had decided to replace debating studies with twice the amount of figure work.

'You will not be able to join your father in business without figure work,' advised his tutors. 'Just because you dislike it is no excuse to shirk.'

'But why must I study what is of no interest to me at the expense of what does interest me?' argued Ni.

'Because that is the way you will become stronger,' they had answered stubbornly. 'Redoubling your efforts on your lesser skills is the only way to remove your weaknesses.'

So, over the next few years, Ni was forced to redouble his efforts, yet, despite working twice as hard, he still received mediocre results. His tutors, however, were pleased to see that he questioned their authority less and less, and that he became more of a critic in the few debates they did allow him *to participate in. They were content when they announced to his father that, in their opinion, Ni was ready to enter business, for they had succeeded in teaching Ni the importance of eliminating weakness.*

'He will be one of your greatest assets,' they told him. 'Your business will continue to grow in strength under your son's careful eye.'

Ni immediately began to replicate the methods he had learned, and for the first time in twenty years his father's business began to lose money.

All of us are mediocre at many things, are good at some, excel at fewer and have the ability to become world class at a few. This is because for every natural strength we are born with, we have countless weaknesses. Having a strength is not the opposite of having a weakness, however. Like success and failure, or health and illness, each follows a particular pattern. But where experiencing failure may be the stumbling block on the natural path to success, seeking improved strength through fixing weakness is very much the wrong path. Fixing weaknesses to improve an individual or business is a fallacy. None the less, it is a practice that is consistently applied throughout schools and all forms of business – to find out what is weak and ensure its removal through concentrated effort. This practice is based on the belief that existing strengths will continue to develop on their own. Therefore, if you want to become the most effective you can be, only spend time on those areas that are holding you back.

Every day the majority of business managers spend time reviewing or appraising others within their control. This is in accordance with the established frame of reference which dominates business thinking – management controls people and things. To control people you monitor their efficiency and effectiveness. The measurement for these elements is the appraisal or review, both good mechanisms, but as the thinking behind them is wrong they are inefficient and ineffective. This is a sweeping yet true statement, as the way they are carried out wastes the time and skill of both appraiser and appraised.

When a company starts out it is able to concentrate on its strengths; once it is established its focus of attention is on correcting its weaknesses. When a child is very young parents are delighted about what their offspring can do; as the child gets older the parents are concerned at what he or she cannot do. Starting school, both parents and teachers focus on discussing what a child is good at. Later, both focus on the lowest marks in a report. The established thinking is firmly set in a frame of reference that is programmed to root out weaknesses in ourselves and others. Consider your habits. Which come to mind first, your bad or your good ones? Next, consider your strengths and weaknesses. Which come to mind first?

With our thinking rooted in improving what's wrong, the majority of our energy is spent in that area. Every day we have a certain amount of energy: physical, emotional, mental and psychic, in ascending order of importance, our psychic energy being the most valuable. When attention is directed to what we can't do, rather than to what we can do, we unwittingly drain ourselves of our psychic energy. Chastising ourselves mentally for being bad at something, for example, will cause us to feel mentally perplexed, emotionally frustrated and physically tired. Conversely, praising ourselves for excelling at something will cause us to be mentally stimulated, emotionally euphoric and physically energetic.

The latter situation is rare, however, because our belief is that if you point out weaknesses and fix them, then everything will be all right. Nothing could be further from the truth, even though your rationale will be shouting at you, saying: 'But you have to know what is wrong, how else can you learn to excel?' The truth is that trying to succeed in an area where you are weak will cause you to develop low self-esteem, a poor self-image and

7

a limited self-ideal. These are the elements that make up your self-concept, the most important command centre you have in your life. Is it any wonder that self-acceptance is lost, when we have been trained to focus our attention on what we must do to correct ourselves, rather than what we can do to excel?

Learning to recognise our few true strengths, and developing the courage to channel our energy into developing them, will transform us into the excellent human beings that the global marketplace in which we operate demands. Those who learn to successfully channel their energy will be the leaders and achievers in their specific fields. Those who don't will continue to feel the inner frustration associated with being unfulfilled. Entrenched thinking cannot simply be eliminated as nature abhors a vacuum. It must be replaced with different thinking, frames of reference that work *for* you, not *against* you. Practising the following keys will strengthen, rather than develop, these frames of reference, because their very application will serve to remind you of their soundness.

SOM Up versus SWOT Down

'You said that these measures would generate growth, yet all they have done is slow up the growth we previously enjoyed,' said a perplexed Hui Neng to his son. 'This past year we have diverted all of our resources into shoring up our weaknesses, as you said it would make us more efficient and our people more effective. But now even Agent Jong has stopped producing.'

'It is simply part of the process,' replied Ni. 'The numerous weaknesses that we have addressed will inevitably make us stronger, but it takes time. As for Agent Jong, I have worked long and hard on improving his figure work, to the point at which his orders can quickly be referenced and measured. They may be less than before, but this is normal. As soon as his productivity in the field increases again, after *his training, he will be a good example to others on how to maintain his figures.'*

'But Jong was my first agent,' said Hui Neng. 'I have known and accepted his methods for years and everyone loves him. Indeed many of our customers are so, only because of Jong. It seems to me that your teaching has impeded him from building his relationships.' Hui Neng paused and looked at his son. He remembered how the young Ni used to love going around with Jong. The agent would say how his son used to talk and laugh with the customers. Something had changed. 'I have a simple philosophy which has always worked,' he continued. 'Work hard, but only at what you love. If struggle is needed, do not do it, for it is not for you. It does not seem right to me for us to spend so much time evaluating our weaknesses and threats.'

'We don't,' argued his son. 'Using the method of analysis that I learned, we look at Strengths, Weaknesses, Opportunities and Threats.'

'That may be the theory, Ni, but the reality is that your whole focus is on our weaknesses and threats. Little time is spent considering what we are good at.'

'That's because we have so many weaknesses and threats!' replied Ni. 'Father, we must correct what we are not good at and concern ourselves with our competitors, or we will be lost.'

Imagine a plain white wall as a metaphor for a well-run, successful business. Now imagine that there is a small black mark somewhere on the wall. Where do you focus your attention? It travels to the blemish. The established thinking of 'let's fix what's wrong' has become so obsessive that we can spot a flaw in seconds, simply because that is what we are looking out for. Whenever someone makes a presentation, we are more attuned to its weaknesses than its strengths. Whenever we meet someone, we are more attuned to evaluating what we dislike about them, rather than what we may like. How many times are we missing the good by habitually searching for the bad?

Take the SWOT analysis, which is applied regularly in

organisational business. Strengths, Weaknesses, Opportunities and Threats are reviewed and considered, yet, without exception, the categories of weakness will take precedence over what is considered strong. Every report will highlight more of the former than the latter in the sincere, albeit misguided, belief that what is wrong must be brought to attention. But it is possible to be sincerely wrong.

In researching what keeps families together, emphasis is placed on resolving the weaknesses that cause break-up, rather than on developing the strengths that bond the family members. Amazingly, all institutional psychology is based on what makes people depressed, rather than on what makes them happy. Opportunities and strengths are given lip service but are not considered worthy of the same discussion time allotted to weaknesses and threats. In the same way that bad habits come to mind before good habits, it is considered wise and prudent to address weaknesses before strengths.

The trouble is that there is never any time to develop the strengths further. This, however, is considered of no great concern, because the erroneous belief is that strengths, left alone, will continue to develop on their own. Far from it. Nature will remove from you whatever you do not use, regardless of the strength of the original gift. Many are born with genius, many with a tendency to write poetry, an inclination to sing, or some other ability. Their gifts vanish, however, if they are starved of use, as do the qualities associated with that gift.

The SWOT analysis can more accurately be termed the 'Seek Weaknesses Only Test'. The manager will spend more time with the salesman over the sales he didn't close, than those he did. He will spend more time with the clerk over the errors he has made rather than discussing the ideas he may have. He will spend more time with the receptionist over procedures of recording than on developing interaction with visitors. Tests are designed to find out what people are not good at, rather than to discover what they are good at. The brilliant practical student is forced to improve his theoretical work, while the brilliant theorist is forced to test his ideas in practical ways which may be out of date. Focusing purely on the strengths of each makes them stronger; focusing on weaknesses makes them weaker. The pragmatist is not a strategist and the strategist is not a pragmatist. Together they are considerably stronger than the one who is forced to be both.

The only way to develop strengths and opportunities is to ignore anything else. Applying the Strengths, Opportunities and Merits analysis, SOM, will focus attention on what is, in the end, the only element of any importance. When you identify your strengths and focus solely on them, your weaknesses do not count. In excelling in what you are brilliant at, your weaknesses become unimportant. Athletes ensure that they only train at what they are good at. In doing so they are remembered for what they can do, rather than what they can't do.

This is not the case in the business arena. Strong cash flow is considered to be the life blood of business, yet it is merely a by-product of the real life blood. The real life blood is strong movement of products or services through strong relationships. Relationships are sustained by people who are good at building them because they like what they do. As the need for these people to become paperwork and technology experts insidiously grows, there is less time to move products and build relationships. The regularity of use of the refrain, 'you can't do that', is indicative of whether a company is focusing on its weaknesses.

Ni was pleased with himself and he knew that his former tutors would also have been pleased. Having invested a great deal of time with Jong and the other agents, he had finally taught them to correctly fill in their expense sheets, their A reports, their B reports and their C reports. And they were doing it on time, or almost. Jong had complained that he'd spent more time on paperwork than on anything else, but Ni had assured him that he would get better at it. Admittedly, income had gone down at first, but that was the marketplace they were in. He had already warned his father that they must diversify rather than specialise, but he would attend to that later. Now, though, income was increasing once more.

'How-so Jong,' hailed Hui Neng, seeing his old friend and agent. 'I see that you are once more winning against the fray. But, hold, why do you look so pleased yet guilty?'

'I am guilty, my Lord, because I hold a secret I would prefer to share with you, yet am loath to do so. I am pleased because the purpose behind the secret is worthy.'

'Then my worthy Jong, share the secret with your friend and the guilt will go.'

So Jong explained how for many months now he had struggled with the elements that Ni had introduced. 'Not just I,' he said, 'but all the others, except for Zhang.'

'Zhang?' commented Hui. 'But he has been the laziest of all my agents.'

'Exactly so,' continued Jong, 'but in the matters of form-filling, the duck has taken to the water. So we all devised a plan. Zhang will do everyone's paperwork, and we have taken over Zhang's area. He receives his full quota, which was more than he received before, and we are free to do what we love and receive our just reward.'

'And I take it that Ni does not know this?' asked Hui. 'No doubt you are concerned that he will insist that you must all do your own.'

'Exactly so, master, which is why I am guilty. I have known Ni for all his years, but he has not the light-heartedness that he carried as a child. It is as though he is obsessed with what makes us weak. Yet our plan, you may recognise, is nothing less than how we began. We work on what we are good at—'

'—because we found that anything we were not good at took twice as *long for half the reward!' finished Merchant Hui. 'I suppose in the beginning our only assets were our strengths, and we sought to embrace every worthwhile opportunity that our strengths opened up. Today our concern has been more on what others do, rather than what we do. What we do to simplify life actually makes it more complex.'*

No-one likes having fault found with what they do, yet everyone has the inclination to do just that with others. The inclination exists because of the belief that, in finding fault, we are being supportive. Although there is nothing fundamentally wrong in a SWOT analysis, it is the application of it that is self-defeating. Applying the SOM analysis strengthens your thinking. Over the next seven days, apply it to whatever you are involved with, as well as to yourself. Only consider strengths and opportunities. Do not even entertain or consider ideas relating to weaknesses or threats of any nature. When appraising another, be they a child, spouse, friend or colleague, ap*praise* their merits, not their faults.

The main point of this exercise is to place the emphasis of your appraisal on improving what you can do, rather than improving what you can't do. Rather than seek to discover why one team does not communicate or perform, seek to discover why another team does, and plan to do more of it. Rather than seek to discover why some people complain, seek to discover why others do not, and follow their example.

When you are conscious of where the emphasis of your thinking is applied, you can then consider weaknesses and threats, as you will place them in their proper perspective – be aware of them so that they do not get in your way. SOMing up rather than SWOTing down allows you to find out what you are good at and do more of it, and to find out what you are not good at so that you can stop doing it. This opens the way to developing the second key. But remember, it is when you juxtapose these simple truths that you complicate your life.

Becoming a Specialist

It is said that the great Sun Tzu was always searching for the world's greatest strategist, right up until he was called to enter the Garden of the Jade Emperor. Indeed, at the very gates the Immortal Guardian, Dragon King Ao-Kuang, welcomed him, exclaiming: 'Ah, Sun Tzu, we have been expecting you. The very person for whom you have searched so long and hard has also recently arrived.'

'Do you actually mean the world's greatest strategist? Who? Where?' asked Sun Tzu immediately.

'Look yonder, the person you seek is just over there,' replied the Immortal Ao-Kuang.

Filled with anticipation and excitement, Sun Tzu turned but what he saw dismayed him. 'But what joke is this? Is this hell's gate I have come to? This man cannot be the person I sought so long and so hard for! He is no warrior or leader of men. He was the general boatman on the River Huai in my home state of Wu, and, so they say, a handyman before that.'

'Because he was good at many things,' said the Immortal Guardian, 'he was often called upon by others, and never got down to doing what he would have excelled at. Had he specialised with the talents he had been given by the Jade Emperor, he would have been the greatest warrior strategist who had ever lived. Artfully manoeuvring the dangerous current and courageously saving the lives of many on the River Huai came easily to him because of his gifts.'

Ni's great uncle, Wei Tzu, paused after telling the story, before adding, 'You see, Ni, had the boatman known about his true strengths, or had they been recognised by another, he would have been able to harness them. Had he been aware of them he would not have spent his life diversifying, he would have focused his energy on becoming the specialist that would have fulfilled his capabilities.'

'You have always spoken wise words, Uncle, but surely what you are saying requires you to put all your eggs in one basket? My scholars were adamant about diversifying, as it helped to spread any risk.'

'Ah,' answered Wei Tzu, 'but how many scholars have ever operated a business, let alone successfully? Experiencing the dark night of the soul is not a theory which can have a model built and applied. Business to many of them is something they test their theories on, making it appear more complex than it actually is. Parents with one child will watch their child more carefully than parents with five children. Each child should be watched the same, but there is not the time unless the family works as a team. If you only have one basket of eggs you are more careful with that basket. When you have eggs in lots of different baskets you are not so concerned if one basket is lost. When you diversify, where do you spend the fixed amount of energy that one day provides? A bit here and a bit there. When you specialise, you apply all your energy. Always put your eggs in one basket, Ni, and guard that basket well, with all of your energy. In that way your eggs will hatch, grow and multiply.'

'But although what you say appears to be sound,' pressed Ni, 'why is it that so many businesses fail? If they had something else to fall back on, they could see their way through hard times.'

'More businesses fail that have diversified than specialised,' answered his great uncle. 'But there are many reasons that businesses fail, the top of which is that people demand more out of something than they are prepared to put in. Many are impatient, and after trying one thing for a short time become bored and apply their energy in another direction. You talk of the need of your father's business to diversify, when its strength is in the speciality it provides. There is of course nothing wrong with diversifying within the specialisation itself, so long as the core skill remains and does not become incidental to the business.

You will find, Nephew, that the strength of a core skill will diminish in proportion to the increase in diversification. A business needs to be nurtured like a child. And the best way to rear a child is to recognise that it is not an extension of yourself, it is an expression of everything that is good about you.'

When you truly express yourself, the world embraces the enthusiasm and commitment you display. It applauds your individuality. When you extend yourself the outcome is not always as you would have hoped for. The key to fully expressing yourself is to find out what you love and to specialise in it to the full. Those who do seek to specialise inevitably discover that the rewards are disproportionate between the best and the rest. Similar to the winning horse whose owner receives ten times more than the owner of the horse that came second, the specialist will reap increasing returns for being the best.

Specialisation is perhaps the single most important factor in evolution itself. Every species has a tendency to seek out its ecological calling and develop its strengths accordingly in order to fulfil itself. Man, however, has a tendency to be influenced by artificial circumstances rather than natural conditions. Thus he seeks to adapt and improvise rather than create and develop.

For example, a person may create a speciality that meets a demand, and develop a niche market which brings rewards. Later, the very dynamics responsible for the speciality and niche are allowed to be influenced by external factors. The somewhat larger organisation that has evolved because of the original speciality and niche becomes concerned about changing markets, competition or recession cycles. Believing that future survival depends on adapting to changing circumstances it decides to diversify. Unwittingly, however, it begins to weaken itself. Instead of reviewing core skills and expressing them in such a way as to meet the changing demands of the marketplace, it involves itself in the areas in which it lacks strength. Where it was once in command, it is now at the mercy of fluctuations in share and interest rates which lie beyond its control. As it expends its energy in concern about elements beyond its control, it becomes increasingly vulnerable.

To specialise, however, does not mean to restrict the possible range of services or products, as long as they are complementary. A bookshop holding a wide range of books is preferable to a bookshop carrying a restricted selection. Where a firm of lawyers may choose to cater for every eventuality that requires law, an individual lawyer who chooses to do so will inevitably be mediocre. Where a mediocre lawyer mistakes being busy for being successful, a specialist lawyer is in demand regardless of his or her fee. Indeed, regardless of the business, when you are competing with a specialist, your profitability will be determined by the service they offer against yours. Knowledge, more now than ever before, is the critical ingredient for attaining leadership, irrespective of the marketplace. Knowledge provides the edge in specialisation to the extent that if you are not continually learning in your specific subject, then whenever you meet another person who is, they will win, and you won't.

The only place to diversify is within the specific specialisation itself, and, even more effective, only diversify through strategic alliances. There can be no finer way to share risk and increase standards through complementary resources than by forging strategic alliances. This involves the building of relationships of which more is discussed under the eleventh scroll. For now, the key to becoming a world class specialist is in channelling your daily energy correctly.

Same Time, Different Choice

The one thing that every person has in common is the amount of time they have in an hour — sixty minutes. Depending on individual priorities, the manner in which these same periods are spent is infinite in choice. Amazingly though, and despite efficient management of time, the majority of our achievement and happiness takes place in a short space of time. Using the unit of one hour as a reference point, ten minutes is utilised in channelling our energy proactively, while fifty minutes is wasted in using our energy reactively. With the majority of our energy absorbed through involvement with such draining elements, it is no surprise that there is so much fatigue and depression.

Every waking hour takes you either towards fulfilling your particular speciality, or away from it. There is no neutral, only forwards or backwards. Channelling your energy has nothing to do with keeping in balance, which is more to do with restoring energy that has been drained. When you channel your energy correctly you actually generate energy; when you do not, you divert energy into frustration, procrastination, exasperation and many other 'ations. Being in balance means having command over the use of your own energy. This requires spending your time only on those activities that you have previously decided are of high value to you. The fact is, however, that we allow what is actually significant to us to be submerged by whatever is insignificant to us.

Deciding what is important in our lives is very much an individual consideration. But as most people do not know what is important in their lives, prioritising can be impossible. The result is the tendency to live vicariously through others; we become more interested in what others are doing than in what we ourselves should be doing. A glance at what dominates daily news reports provides ample testament to this tendency.

Applying the rule of 'it is not the hours you put in, it is what you put in the hours', consider the following. Do your waking hours involve: thinking about what you should have done; worrying about what you should be doing; doing things other people have asked you to do and which you couldn't say no to; doing things you don't enjoy; doing things that are interrupted; doing things you are not very good at; doing things that are part of a ritual; doing things that are predictable; doing things in order to put off what you have planned to do; daydreaming about what you would like to be doing?

But that's just the way life is, you may be thinking to yourself. To spend time the way you want, or for that matter ought, is just not feasible. Your work does not allow you the freedom to do otherwise, or you would have to be single to live the way you want. In any case, you think, one must not be selfish. Wrong.

However you rationalise it you will not detract from the reality of the way you currently employ your energy. Becoming a specialist requires more than mere discernment. It demands a ruthlessness in saying no to anything that you intuitively feel is draining your energy. This requires an honesty with yourself as to what is important in your life, for it is only with such honesty that you can be honest with others. In turn this involves establishing ground rules with those you share your life with. Treating others as you yourself would want to be treated, by definition involves thinking of what is right for you first, for when you are on course the ripple effect that exudes from you is beneficial to others.

Applying this Golden Rule does not mean you should compromise what is important to you, however, for seeking to please others just so that they will not think ill of you can build resentment and guilt.

It is, of course, difficult to cut out activities that take you away from what you want, when you are uncertain as to *what* it is you *do* actually want. But knowing what you want, and doing what you enjoy, are the very pillars of specialisation success. This leads us to the next vitally important key.

Following a Calling

'Running a business is like riding a tiger,' said Merchant Hui Neng to his son. 'There is immense strength and power within your hands and, as you pound through the jungle, your blood races with adrenaline. If you drive the tiger too hard, you run the risk of riding it into the ground, burning out all of its energy. If you ride it too softly, your attention weakens and the tiger, as if sensing your lack of direction, may unexpectedly spring in a different direction, where the jungle is even denser. If you stop, though, the tiger may turn and maul you, leaving you in pieces.'

'I have learned, Father,' said Ni, 'about the importance of developing strengths and of specialising, but how can one ride a tiger without rest, as you say, and still maintain balance?'

'By having a calling, developing a passion and learning to communicate it to others in such a way that they want to support you,' the merchant answered. 'When you are able to align what you do with what you are, you build for yourself unyielding support.'

'But surely only idealists have callings,' said Ni, 'and they are usually empty.'

'That may appear to be so because having a personal mission is so rare,' replied Hui. 'It is rare because society does not promote it, and it does not do so because it does not understand its importance. Goals to further develop our careers are promoted, but rarely are they encapsulated within the framework of a personal calling. Yet each person's calling, my son, will be the very

essence of why they do what they do. The idealist is the sincere individual who follows his ideal, regardless of how others perceive it. A calling is what throws light on the path of life and what gives interest to life. Tell me: if a man does not live for an ideal, what does he live for?'

'For himself, I suppose,' Ni answered.

'Exactly so, and when he lives for himself, he lives for nothing. Whosoever lives and knows not an ideal, is without power and without light. A sincere ideal, no matter how small, is an ideal. The greater the ideal, the greater the person; the deeper the ideal, the deeper the person; and the higher the ideal, the higher the person. Without ideal, calling or mission, whatever the person is in life, their life is causeless.

'Always remember, Ni, to follow your heart by encapsulating everything that you stand for, everything that is important to you, and everything that is worthwhile to you, into your own personal calling. And, if you do not yet know what that calling is, then make it your first cause to discover it. Hunt your own tiger, mount it and then ride for all you are worth.'

There is nothing more personally motivating, more energy building, more fulfilling and more worthwhile, than knowing that what you do is what is important to you, is what holds meaning for you, is what you want to do, and, above all, is what you are inclined to do.

The best way to channel your energy is to develop your strengths; the best way to develop your strengths is to build them within the framework of your own personal mission. Having a calling and following it gives purpose to life and meaning to what you do. Without a personal calling your energy will flow into the countless tributaries of materialistic goals, all of which will sap your strength in due course.

To live and breathe is to be created for a purpose, and to discover and fulfil that purpose is to realise our potential. Moreover, each of us has a responsibility and a duty to be extravagant with our potential, for why else would it be given to us? Absorbing ourselves in something bigger and grander than ourselves provides the opportunity to fully develop and share our strengths. Having a clear purpose allows us to believe in ourselves and know what we stand for; it's about deciding what business you are in as a person. In the same way that you would not have confidence in a business that didn't know what it stood for, why should a company have confidence in an individual who doesn't know what he or she stands for? If you don't know what you stand for, you are continually pulled betwixt and between anything else that comes along.

Discovering your calling and developing it with accompanying values means sticking to a process. This in itself is difficult, as it is both emotionally and spiritually searching. Anything worthwhile does require effort, of course, but it removes the feeling of continual yet futile struggle, as it turns a sense of longing into a sense of belonging. The process requires deep and reflective time alone as only your own intuitive self can provide the answers. By all means crystallise your thinking in discussions with others, so long as you remember that family, friends and colleagues are agencies, not sources. For a mission to be personal it has to encapsulate the passion of your own vision, not someone else's. Be aware of aligning yourself to something to please or impress others. Too many people live by scripts which have been handed to them by others, with no contribution by themselves.

In asking and answering questions to discover your calling it is important to be aware of being yourself. This means being honest and true to yourself without allowing any rationalisation to cloud your thinking. To the degree that you are yourself, you become receptive to understanding what you are to do. To the degree that you are not true to yourself, you are closed to what you are to do. In answering questions such as 'what difference is my life going to have made?' and 'what would I want others to say of me when I'm gone?', you must be your honest self.

However long it takes, aim to develop a meaningful statement that will galvanise your strengths and talents. Clarify what values are central to your life and work, and ensure that they are reflected in your personal goals, relationships with others, the commitments and promises you make, and the kind of preferences you hold. Established values take the tension out of those 'will I, won't I' dilemmas. The process of crystallising your calling in a meaningful statement may take hours, weeks or months. You will also need to regularly review it, but do persevere as the quest for meaning and purpose in your life is far too important to be just fitted in, or to be treated as a task on a 'to do' list. Remember that your calling is something that every fibre of your being yearns for, that excites you emotionally, motivates you mentally and fulfils you spiritually. As such it is of paramount importance.

Having a statement of what is important to you allows you to align what you do with what you are. It qualifies you to assist in developing or reviewing a mission for your company, or the organisation in which you work, with new understanding and appreciation. It is nothing less than the highest form of arrogance, even ignorance, to criticise the mission of another without having gone through the process of developing your own first. Yet, in seeking to spot the flaw first, the majority of people spend more time knocking the ideals or missions of others, even of those they work with, with cynical remarks.

Spending time developing a personal mission and understanding individual values, rather than criticising the suggestions of others over a charter of shared purpose, allows the alignment of individual values, beliefs and philosophy with a company. People who take the time to do this naturally view things from a different perspective. They may choose to leave, or they may choose to be proactive rather than reactive. The principle of putting your own house in order before complaining about the state of the street is a good one to follow. Just one person who genuinely cares about the direction of the company they work with can begin to make a significant difference, regardless of their station. People want meaning in their lives, it is the essential ingredient in organisational success.

Having and following a calling is exhilarating as it begins to permeate everything you do, shaping your actions and building your relationships. By creating and continually reviewing what you are all about, what really absorbs and interests you, you ensure that you utilise your strengths to the full and perform to your best each day, a best that continually improves.

Guardian of Energy

In the same way that we are capable of holding a desire because we have the God-given abilities to achieve it, each of us has a specific calling which our inherent strengths are perfectly designed to serve. That is the reason for our strengths, their very intent. Strengths, talents and natural skills, or lack of them, are expressions of the way our inner force manifests itself. Each of us is pure energy and it is our responsibility how we direct our energy. If we allow others to drain our energy, then we must accept responsibility for allowing it to happen. Similarly, whenever we involve ourselves in something that is of no interest to us, then we must be aware, as well as accept, that we are not utilising ourselves in a manner that will ever bring fulfilment.

By focusing on what we can do, through being conscious of our strengths, by recognising those opportunities that appeal to us, by becoming a specialist in what we naturally excel in and are good at, and by following a calling that means the world to us, each of us will consciously, and unconsciously, gravitate to that which holds meaning for us and directs us in channelling our energy.

The tiger-cub howled as it limped home. 'I am never going to spring and jump again,' he complained to his father.

'But that is what you are naturally good at,' his father consoled, then playfully bowling over the young cub with his immensely powerful paw, added, 'Do you not enjoy it?'

'Not any more!' cried the cub. 'I put everything into that last jump and all I get is hurt for my trouble.'

'My son, you are a guardian of all the special strength and power that is contained within you. As guardian you must learn how to channel it, for such energy, when misdirected, will otherwise hurt you. Your energy has no limitations, other than the ones you allow it to have. Just because you have hurt yourself once or twice in trying, does not mean that you will always do so. You must persevere.

'When you next spring and jump, first contain your energy, becoming aware of just how much you will need and why you are about to use it. As you do, you will feel the energy build up inside you until, when the moment feels just right, you let it go. At that moment you will experience your body, mind and energy flowing as one unit. Then you will no longer be jumping, you will be flying through the air. And the air itself will be with you, riding the tiger.'

The Second Scroll: Knowing the Eagle

The Secret of Realising Your Desires
While Needing Nothing

Hermit Yen glimpsed three eagles soaring above him. Calling them down to him he requested of the first, 'How much to carry me across the plains to the neighbouring state, please?'

'It's a two-day flight at least and you are a heavy load,' replied the first eagle. 'I would like ten fish, a goat and a flagon of soya milk.'

'So much,' said Hermit Yen, and turning to the second eagle asked, 'What will you do it for?'

'It is right you are a heavy load,' answered the second eagle, 'yet as I am due to go in that direction in any case, I would want five fish, a kid-goat and a flagon of rice-water. It is a long trip that will require sustenance.'

Asking the third eagle what the charge would be, the hermit was surprised to hear, 'Five fish and a litre of water.'

'What kind of fool answer is that?' Yen shouted. 'Why do you possibly ask for an amount that will not even sustain you for the trip?'

'I needed the order,' said the crestfallen eagle.

'Needed the order!' the hermit returned angrily. 'Well my desire to go will not be at the mercy of your need. In compromising your worth you compromise my life! Come,' the hermit said to the second eagle, 'let us plan

27

our trip. With your desire to go my way and your considered charge, I know my journey is assured.'

The Polarities of Desire

Healthy desire is the starting point of all achievement. The desire to live, for instance, is the unconscious motivation to take our first breath of life. There are, however, polarities to our desires, so that, depending on how much we want something, we can unwittingly bring about adverse conditions. A simple illustration of this is the ambitious individual, who, desiring to impress others, brings about the opposite effect.

Our desires attract to us the elements which make us what we are and form our behaviour. The experiences we encounter in our lives, therefore, come from what we consciously or unconsciously attract to us. Every living thing displays a peculiarity because it has attracted a particular element to become so. The insect living in the mud displays different qualities to the insect living in the beautiful flower. The soaring eagle displays different qualities to the tiny sparrow. Man, who is the finished specimen of creation, reveals this doctrine in its fullness. His successes and failures, his sorrows and joys, all depend on what he desires and what he has desired for himself. It is the nature of his intent behind those desires that counts.

The question then arises: 'why would I want to desire elements which are undesirable to me, such as failure and sorrow?' The answer is that you did not desire them as you see them now, but as you saw them before. One does not seek pain purposely, one seeks pleasure, yet very often pain is hiding behind the façade of pleasure. Similarly, a seeker of success may not see failure hiding behind what he believes to be success.

Desires spawned from a false self lead to false activity and subsequent discomfort. One who desires a partner for the sake of parental pressure, appearance, security, jealousy, obsession, infatuation, habit or loneliness, will soon discover pain behind short-lived pleasure. Another who desires success for the sake of promotion, acquisition, status, title, money, respect or receiving credit, will similarly experience a hollowness to their rewards.

As the whole principle of creation is based on the power of intent, it is important to think and understand what you want and why you want it. When you enter into business with another, you must know the philosophy of your partner. When young people are in love, the intensity of their passion blinds their respective philosophies. With the short-term need gained through either alliance, long-term limitations to deeper desires are overlooked. In complaining to ourselves that we never receive what we consider we are duly entitled to, there can be no end to our complaining. Unconsciously we are, in effect, desiring something to complain about. Therefore, in order to have no complaints, we must become aware when and why we complain.

In desiring things, we must distinguish, at each step in life, what we must manifest for ourselves and what we must not manifest for ourselves. Our lives are decided by our innermost pictures, generated by what we might wittingly, or unwittingly, desire from life. Fortune is not external, it is decided by how you desire it.

The Importance of Desire

Desire is a form of energy linked to our lower physical and higher mental energies. Only when desire is out of balance with the higher energy functions of the mind, and serves the lower instead, does trouble follow. Out of physical desire, for example, a person may lose their calmness and clarity of mind and be compelled to act against their better judgement.

The fact is, however, nature has designed desire and its proper use as one of the most important elements of life. Implanted in every living being is a strong desire for that which is necessary for well-being, nourishment and growth. Where perhaps spirituality gains release, for example, religion seeks control, and in censoring Man against the curse of having desires, has metaphorically speaking thrown the baby out with the bath water. Many people counteract their desires with guilt, particularly in regard to relationships and wealth.

The importance of desire is such that with its power you already have the capacity to manifest, or attract, whatever you want in your life. The very fact you have a 'desire', the Latin root of which translates as 'of the father', means that you have the God-given ability to achieve it. In other words, you would be incapable of holding a desire unless you had the capability to create its reality. Although most of what we are taught to believe conflicts with this, your desires are the very tools that assist you in expressing your purpose. It is because of false indoctrination, however well-meaning, that the art of manifesting our desires for positive benefit has been forgotten.

The Four Keys of Your Higher Desire Power

The Higher Self is simply another title for the stronger, truer and real you, who, although never absent, is seldom paid attention to. When something just right for you arrives out of the blue, for instance, it is because your Higher Self is acting in the interests of your honest desires. It is of course easier to believe that it is simply luck, coincidence, or 'too good to be true', which is why opportunities are often ignored. Because your Higher

Desire Power always operates indirectly, it causes you to take the longest way round as the quickest way for you to attain your desire. If necessary, therefore, it will cause your well-laid plans to be overturned, resulting in you thinking that failure and defeat, rather than success and victory, have come to you.

Often it will have to tear you away from your existing, seemingly comfortable, circumstances, and throw you between a rock and a hard place in order to let you see the success it has attained for you. A characteristic of highly successful individuals is that they have experienced 'the dark night of the soul'. As one who has experienced finally ending up on the right track said, 'It took my whole world to cave in before I could see that the success I craved was beneath my feet. I was just walking in the shoes of someone I felt I should be, rather than wanted to be.' Although their previous false activities brought it on themselves, genuinely successful people always agree that the price paid was well worth it.

It is usually because the four keys essential to channel your Higher Desire Power are never utilised that it is forced to take the action it does. How else can it realise your desires, which is its sole function, if you insist on building the frustration within you by virtue of being on the wrong track? Your Higher Self freely employs the faculties of the subconscious and the collective conscious in its work to magnetically draw towards you what you ardently desire. It is not creating something for you, it is manifesting what already exists for you.

Uninfluenced by the distractions Man fills his life with, homing pigeons, migrating birds and animals lost over long distances successfully home in on what they want. Anyone establishing a sanctuary for birds will tell you that even the strangest of species, indigenous to other countries, will soon begin to travel towards it. High or low, the Higher Self will manifest its power. Man can harness Desire Power in the same way that he has successfully harnessed other great natural forces available to him, through application of the following four practices.

Accepting Your Worthiness to Receive

The brothers Po and Jo of Sung were inseparable as youths. Po dreamed of success as a merchant while Jo had resigned himself to the monastic tradition of his ancestors.

'Please do not enter commerce,' Jo entreated his brother, 'for the ways of business will make you unworthy to enter the Garden of the Jade Emperor and we will no longer be together.'

'It is not the ways of business that makes one unworthy, it is how much one allows one's self to be influenced by the needful habits of others. Anyway, learning to recognise such things may lead to the worthy cause of influencing others positively — who knows, I may run a state in time?'

'But you know as well as I do,' persisted Jo, 'that abundance and spirituality are incompatible. Both our elders and parents have always taught us to believe that it is both selfish and improper to visualise and desire success and material things. Already I fear that your ambition places you above your station.'

Six months after being persuaded by his brother's relentless admonitions to follow him, Po was talking to a visiting traveller.

'I would have liked to enter commerce, but it was an unworthy desire and I realised it was only for selfish reasons,' said Po, in answer to a question posed by the traveller.

'Nonsense! When you deny your desire to follow a particular path,' said the traveller, 'you deny yourself as the spiritual being you are. You cannot blame your brother's seemingly selfish action for making you feel unworthy about getting what you want and guilty for wanting it. Whatever you have, you allow yourself to have. Understand that what you really want matters, because that is what becomes matter. Material form is how the spirit of all

things makes itself known to us. It is not selfish to want whatever you do in life and you should not be ashamed when what you want happens.'

'But it's too late. Everyone is content that I am a humble monk now. It is not worthy for me to receive what I once longed for.'

'It is true that what you receive is proportionate to what you believe you are worth, but never say that others made you into what you are today,' said the traveller. *'Accept that you chose instead to acquiesce to the demands of others. From this moment say to yourself that you will be willing to accept full responsibility for whatever you bring into your life. Doing so will automatically place you in the position of becoming increasingly worthy to attract and receive whatever you desire.'*

Awakening, Po realised that there had been no traveller, he had simply been dreaming. Sharing his dream with the Patriarch of his brotherly order, he was counselled to 'follow your heart's desire, for in so doing you become worthy of it and it becomes worthy of you. Everyone's path is different, yet only a few ever recognise the integrity of a true desire, and in doubting it, cause themselves to become unworthy to receive it.'

Following his dream Po became a successful trader and, in time, his worth was recognised by Duke Mu of Ch'in, who made him his high minister.

Too often we allow the conditioned beliefs and admonitions of others who have low self-regard, to exert influence and power over us. In doing so we put on the clothes that validate the unworthiness that for so long has adorned them. Thinking that success and riches are incompatible with spirituality, for example, is one of the largest contributors to feeling unworthy.

It is a sad fact that the amount of self-worth a child feels reduces dramatically during its formative years. Whenever children are able to resist the consistent hypnosis of being limited in their abilities, they are able to express their unlimited selves and manifest the abundance and opportunity they want throughout their lives. But it is, of course, impossible for most children to resist the ideas and limiting beliefs of their surrounding influences. Adhering to a curriculum of teaching to get by in life, rather than get on in life, the emphasis, unwittingly, is on reducing self-worth, thereby limiting the child's potential rather than releasing it. Most teachers and parents will freely admit that although they recognise that praise develops growth, the emphasis is on correcting mistakes.

It is therefore vital, as adults, to accept personal responsibility for redeveloping our worthiness to receive. This means acknowledging that our self-esteem comes from ourselves, not from others; accepting ourselves without complaint and refusing to allow guilt into our lives.

Anything that promises worthwhile results is easier said than done, but, as personal development programmes are almost non-existent both at school, where we spend a good part of life learning, and in the work environment, where we spend a much greater part, it is up to every individual to be accountable to themselves. Being accountable involves taking ownership as well as responsibility over your own growth. It is acknowledging that empowerment does not come from others, because you can only empower yourself. When you know that you alone are responsible for how you choose to react to every life situation and stop blaming others, your shift in consciousness increases your worthiness to receive.

To accept yourself does not mean to accept every conditioned behaviour, which can be altered, but it does mean to stop mentally chastising yourself and putting yourself down. Self-repudiation is in disharmony with your Higher Self, as are persistent feelings of guilt that prevent you from manifesting anything worthwhile, and instead attract to you the very same things about which you are sending out messages.

In refusing to allow former conditioning to dictate the limits of what you deserve in life, you automatically allow yourself to accept the abundance and opportunity that is available for you.

Applying Your 'Rightness' for Receiving

Yuan Wen was a merchant of jade. His business was to take intricate and beautiful adornments to the houses of people who liked to buy. One day he was sharing his business psychology with his friend, Wei Tzu.

'In the trade of jade there is great scope for dishonesty, yet every day I am further convinced of a spiritual truth while doing my business. Most days I take my gems for people to see, I honestly tell them the price and mostly I see that they are sold, and profit by it.

'However, it is hard to always be a saint in business. Sometimes I have felt that a customer is really attracted to an item and, sensing his want, I have added a little more to the price. But in doing so, it seems that I was robbed of some power, and experienced a sense of loss during the day. This is no coincidence, for not just once but many times this has happened. It seems that whenever temptation robbed that sacred power within me, then that day I was not successful in my business.'

'I too will admit to this experience in past times,' said Wei Tzu to his friend. 'What does this show us? It shows us that hidden within our heart is a Divine Power, that is developed by keeping what we attract to ourselves in harmony with what we want. Whenever we allow need, greed or speed to influence our desires, they are distorted and come back to us with a sense of emptiness. This in turn leads to a change in our attitude and behaviour which others sense and either reflect back to us or cause them to become suspicious and disinterested.'

The degree to which your areas of thinking, feeling and behaviour are not in harmony is in direct proportion to your ability to attract what you really want. This means examining the attitudes that you knowingly, and unknowingly, hold about your life.

Your attitudes are expressions of the way you think, the very frames of reference you have constructed to support your world. It follows that if matter is thought made concrete, then your thoughts are the architects of your material world, and your attitudes the builders. If you have thoughts about how you want to conduct your life and then behave in a manner that does not reflect this 'rightness', ultimately you become self-defeating in your ability to manifest.

Life is full of temptations to test our 'rightness' attitude. Our tendency is to constantly complain about our conditions. Yet, if we were immediately placed in the conditions we so desired, rather than feel satisfaction we would soon feel the scarcity in those conditions also. This is because we seek only to fulfil our outer needs, which do not satisfy the emptiness within us. The question arises, therefore, of how we can reach harmony with the conditions of life when they conflict with our desires.

Those who complain most about life and who are the most disappointed and troubled will inevitably struggle the most, whatever their conditions. Such complaining reduces our ability to apply our rightness to receive. A condition as bitter as poison can be turned into nectar by getting in rhythm with it, and this can only be done with a rightness of attitude. When experiencing a period of favourable conditions, a person will fear for the time it will end, and will even ask, 'Yes, but how long will it last?' Yet, when experiencing an adverse period they do not think of when it will end, rather they wallow and complain about it and wonder, 'Oh dear, what is to become of us?' This is illustrated by the fact that bad news travels along a business grapevine five times faster than good news.

The very nature of life, from morning through to evening, is that everything changes, so why should we not believe that bad times will change and good times will come? In allowing ourselves to fall into the habit of expecting the worst, we directly affect our attitudes and desires. In doing so we generate fear and agitation which only serve to get us further out of rhythm with our condition.

Many imaginative and intelligent people who read every little struggle in the daily newspapers allow themselves to believe that the world is falling to pieces. Others, whose own world is currently in pieces will exclaim, 'What am I to do?' And if their world is not in pieces, they will still conclude that 'it will be harder to survive in the future.' A few will not concern themselves as they forge ahead, despite the ups and downs going on around them, while at the other end of the scale, another few extremists will conclude that astronomical signs, such as an approaching comet, portend the end of the world and end their own lives.

When your attitudes and desires are misguided, because you have the opportunity to get away with something, or because you rationalise that a particular difficult condition warrants such an attitude, your ability to receive is distorted. By ensuring that your attitudes and desires are right you become in rhythm with your Higher Desire Power. Consequently, you are guided to that which is right for you regardless of the conditions that life presents.

Developing Your Prosperity Consciousness

Four merchants met on the road to Tai Kwok market. After initial pleasantries they began to ask each other why prosperity shone on some and not others.

'It is wealth that makes life run smoothly,' said the first. 'Yet despite my good efforts I never have any, and I am continually fraught. So, for my part, I am certain that to receive prosperity, you must first have wealth.'

'Having wealth is not the difficulty,' said the second, 'it is keeping it that I find so hard. The more I try to hang on to my wealth, the more it

seems to diminish. So, for my part I am certain that to have prosperity, you must first keep it.'

'Keeping wealth is not the difficulty,' said the third, 'it is the making more of it, while keeping what you have, that I find so hard. Despite making more it never seems to provide me with enough. So, for my part, I am certain that to keep prosperity, you must first make it.'

'Having, keeping or making wealth is of no consequence to receiving prosperity,' said the fourth, 'it is whether your thinking is one of abundance or one of need. So, for my part, I am certain that it is not your purse that makes you rich or poor. It is your thinking, and it is only abundant thinking that will cause prosperity to shine upon you.'

Generally, when people don't have, they think about not having; when they have, they think about how not to lose it; and when they keep it safe, they think about how there is never enough. Therefore, people who are worried about not having enough allow it to infect their consciousness so much that they merely endorse the insecurity that denies prosperity.

Those who need things are at the mercy of a scarcity mentality. Most people, as well as the majority of businesses, suffer from this, although they are unaware of it. Often seemingly successful in spite of themselves, their competitive outlook actually limits them. The need of an individual for a greater income is no different from the need of a company for greater turnover and profits. After all, the actions employed in running a business are the expressed thoughts of the individuals that fuel it.

Consistent growth and increasing profits are, of course, a healthy benchmark of business. Indeed, without profit there can be no business. But the 'need' outlook takes the view that when a slice of the market pie is taken, there is less of the pie to enjoy. The rarer 'abundant' outlook takes an entirely different view. For example, just because one person is fluent in a language does not mean that another cannot learn, for there is plenty of vocabulary for everyone.

If you think poor you will stay poor, because your thinking is focused on what is not wanted. Ask anyone what they want in a relationship, in business or in life, and it soon reveals how they view their world. When they say, 'Let me tell you about what I don't want in a relationship' or 'I know what I don't like about business', then you can be fairly certain that they are suffering from a scarcity consciousness, and will normally believe they never have enough.

Developing an 'abundant' outlook means not having to think about your needs. It means establishing your wants and thinking only about those. Thinking abundantly is accepting that there is a natural course to obtaining what you want. It will require effort, but not struggle. Whenever you experience yourself struggling with something, be assured that it is not for you. Moreover, if you continue to struggle you are putting yourself in the world of the needy. On the other hand, healthy effort, however fervent, which leaves you feeling that what you are doing is worthwhile and important, is definitely for you. It is vital that these alternatives are recognised, as the former means you are operating from a scarcity mentality, whereas the latter confirms you are operating from an abundance mentality.

Dependent on your thinking is your propensity to attract or repel prosperity. To develop a wealth consciousness is to never again think about what you lack, and about what others lack, and to never view the success of another as confirmation of your lack of luck. Rather, whenever you hear news of a friend, relative or colleague who has done well, use their success as confirmation that there is infinite abundance for you also.

Begin to accept, both intellectually and emotionally, that any scarcity thinking has originated and developed, either consciously or unconsciously, from listening and being influenced by others. Then allow your thinking to accept, both intellectually and emotionally, the image of abundance in your life as being perfectly natural. Doing this for just a few days will make you aware of how a shift in your thinking will alter your expectations. This, in turn, leads us to the most important of the four keys.

Letting Go of What You Want

'At last,' Tung Kuo said to himself, 'with this latest commission how splendidly I will be able to live!' In orchestrating the negotiations for Master Tien to take over the Ch'ien Low business of Yueh he had excelled himself. All the work was done and he simply had to wait. In six months the Registrar of Yueh would ratify the deal with the Ruler's Seal.

As the time went by all he could think about day and night was how he would be able to fulfil all his desires. There were many luxuries he had decided on, he could settle all his debts and, more significantly, his status among his peers would rise.

'Why do you not work these past five months?' colleagues would ask. 'Has the deal you live for come off already?'

'It will any day now so my time is fully taken up in getting ready for when it does,' replied Tung Kuo excitedly.

Why couldn't his family be so excited? he thought to himself. His uncle had advised against becoming so attached to a future event — could he not realise how important this was?

'But it is the security I have been desiring for so long,' he had argued.

'Your desire for security is good, but it will not come from attention to the future, it comes from attention to the present,' his uncle had replied. 'Beware of attaching your emotional energy to something in the future or you will become like a prisoner bound with the chains of anticipation. You have sent your desires out, now detach yourself from their outcome or the price of freedom may be costly to you.'

Rather than let go Tung Kuo tied himself up in emotional knots as the time when he would hear news of the deal's conclusion drew nearer. He became increasingly impatient and irritated with everyone he spoke to and had no time to think about anything else. Family, colleagues and creditors getting on with their own daily functions, kept out of his way.

Receiving a letter from Master Tien close to the appointed day, he excitedly tore it open. The message was to inform him that due to the sudden assassination of the Ruler by the men of Yueh, it was not possible for the Registrar to ratify the sale of Ch'ien Low's estate. Indeed, the letter added, both the Registrar and Seal had been removed from office.

Tung Kuo never fully recovered from the stroke that he instantly suffered on reading the letter. It was some time later that his family were able to inform him about the further news received the very same day. Master Tien had omitted to say in his first letter that as both Ch'ien Low and he still wanted to proceed, albeit recognising it would have to be much later, he would still pay commission. An alliance had been agreed with a much lower price, so whenever Tung Kuo wished to present himself at the House of Tien, he would receive payment.

Whenever you are about to say something and a distraction in the conversation causes you to forget whatever it was, experience tells you that the act of forgetting it brings it back. What you want to impart to another may be on the tip of your tongue, but the more you refuse to let it go, the more elusive it becomes. It is the act of letting go that allows you to recall it. If it comes to you much later, rather than earlier, it is because it took you longer to relinquish it.

It comes to you because your attention is occupied with something that is relevant to the present moment, such as driving. As long as your attention is in the present, then your intent for the future will manifest itself. The real power behind fulfilling a desire is your intention, because intent is desire without attachment to the outcome.

In creating a garden you would not consider pulling up

recently planted flower seeds to see if they are growing, yet the tendency with the seeds of desire is to become emotionally attached to them. In doing so you are centering your attention on a specific result in the future. In order to manifest whatever it is you want in your life, you have to be able to let go of your emotional attachment to the outcome.

This is a metaphysical ordinance. Holding on to things disturbs the manifestation of your desire, so that even if what you want comes through, it will be distorted. This is because there are infinite possibilities available in the way in which your unmanifest desire can be expressed as a manifest reality. This uncertainty allows your desire, sent out by your intent, to return to you in a form that may even exceed your expectations.

The level of energy and rate of vibration that the desire created by your intent emits, will seek correlation with the vibration that matches the desire and bring it to you. Your detachment from any outcome accelerates the natural process of creation, whereas your attachment to it freezes your desire, impeding the fluidity of your intent's vibration, thus breaking the process.

Springing from poverty consciousness, attachment is based on the fixed belief that security will be gained through external symbols that validate the individual desiring them. Material goals and objectives that are worthwhile and bring benefit to us are a healthy part of personal development and a positive measure to monitor growth, but they must never be viewed as providing the security that people constantly seek. The fact is that the search for security outside of ourselves will always elude us, and at best remain short-lived. Attachment to money, for example, will always create insecurity regardless of the amount.

Getting wound-up because you feel the need to attain certain symbols, whether in the form of titles, status or money, makes you the slave of your desires rather than the master of them.

Think about what it is you currently desire. The level of your emotional attachment to its outcome will be indicated by how frustrated you feel by it not happening yet, and how much you feel compelled to force, or think about forcing, a solution.

Detachment, on the other hand, is born of a wealth consciousness, because when what you desire has no hold over you, you are free to create whatever you want. One of the best examples of realised desire and detachment is allowing the child you've nurtured to the best of your ability, under your earnest intent for their well-being and happiness, to live their own life without feeling any impediment from your emotional attachment and judgement of them. The major reason for conflict within families is when emotional attachment, expressed via control, becomes the form of security.

Similarly, one of the major reasons for conflict both in individuals and business is the forcing of solutions in order to fulfil a need. It is easy to see that the scenario of desiring to exceed all expectations in the way you perform, harnesses your power. Yet the opposing scenario of needing something at all costs, which compromises your power, usually predominates.

Your desire to improve your lifestyle by wanting a better car, promotion or more business, for example, indicates your innate power to be able to bring it into your life. But an emotional attachment to whatever it is you desire will immediately and significantly diminish this power and allow all manner of debilitating emotions to gnaw away at you. Letting go of an outcome does not require you to compromise your values or objectives and, moreover, will ultimately bring to you what you want. Not letting go, however, will cause you to incur force and stress that will compromise more than your outcome; you will compromise your health.

The great eagle, its huge wings covering its craggy mountain eyrie, was not immediately aware of losing one of her young as she tried to protect them from the fierce storm. The mother hen in the farm below was similarly unaware that something had dropped into the soft hay of her coop.

Reared to behave as a chicken, the young eagle never learned to fly, completely unaware that his nature was to be a king among birds. A passing hermit noticed him awkwardly holding his great wings while he strutted and pecked with the other chickens.

'Don't you know what you are?' said the hermit, gently taking the eagle in his arms. 'Your nature is to soar the skies. Come, stretch forth your wings and fly.'

The hermit's action confused the eagle, however, as he did not know who he was, and he jumped down to rejoin the chickens. For several days the hermit persisted, each time taking the eagle to higher ground, saying, 'Know that although you may live like a chicken, inside you beats the heart of an eagle, a great eagle, know that you are the king of birds. Go, stretch forth your wings and fly.' But each time, the eagle appeared unaware of his true, unknown self, and awkwardly hopped back to join the chickens who were scratching for corn in the dust. The hermit noticed, though, how the eagle would cast a few glances at the sky, almost as if sensing something stir deep within his heart.

Finally the hermit carried the bird to the top of the mountain. Reaching a steep crag far above the chicken coop, the hermit held the bird aloft while repeating his words of encouragement. 'Out there, among the heavens is where you belong. Go now! Stretch forth your wings and fly! Become the eagle that you are.'

But still the bird did not accept his true power. Not knowing what to do, the eagle's powerful vision swept back and forth from his coop to the sky. He could see the chickens pecking at their food, and felt that he needed to be back there. Then, as if spying something far in the distance, he began to tremble and slowly stretched out his wings. It seemed to the hermit that the eagle was growing in stature and, just at the moment when he could no longer hold him, the great eagle let out a triumphant cry and soared into the heavens.

In letting go of what it had been conditioned to need, the eagle was able to gain its heart's desire, although attachment to what it considered its security to be prevented it from immediately knowing this. None of us were born to scratch out our needs in the dust. Yet, in forgetting our true identity, many of us cede our immense power for realising our desires in favour of the needs that circumstances and conditioning dictate for our security.

Accepting our worthiness and applying our rightness to receive whatever we desire, means knowing what we want and why we want it. Developing our prosperity consciousness as to how we receive, and having the courage to let go of our emotional attachment to whether we receive, means acknowledging the power of our true selves.

Like the great eagle, we can desire everything, while needing nothing. It is the ability to let go of what you think you need that gives you the power to realise your desires.

The Third Scroll: Awaiting the Turtle

The Secret of Being in the Right Place
at the Right Time

'The opportunity for human life is rare,' began the Patriarch, Wei Tzu. 'So rare that it can be likened to that magical event which occurs just once every four hundred years. The moment when the great mythical sea turtle rises for air. Imagine, that while breaking the surface, the creature places its head through a bamboo ring. A hoop that happens to be floating randomly alone in the vast ocean. What perfect timing that would take! Imagine too that this solitary wooden necklace fitted exactly. What precision that would be! Now imagine that the human physical body is the bamboo circle, and the turtle is the immortal spirit entering it. Then you can imagine the perfect coming together of forces that must happen for our own birth.'

'It is indeed hard to consider that our life is such a rarity,' replied his pupil, Lu Chou. 'Just look at the countless people going about their business in the Imperial city each day!'

'Just so,' answered Wei Tzu, 'and each one of them is just where they should be. For in truth our lives are the result of a synchronicity between the physical and spiritual. As such each one of us began our lives at the rightly appointed time, and in the correct place.'

'That must be why one person's timing in life seems infinitely better *than another's' commented Lu Chou. 'Where one man seems to make his fortune, another does not; where one struggles to no avail, another seems to attain easily.'*

'That is not the reason,' said the Patriarch, 'for the time and place has nothing to do with a man's success. The rightness and timing in awaiting the turtle is merely to illustrate that such synchronicity is our birthright. But Man, instead of resolving to continue to use this natural serendipitous power, has become conditioned to do the opposite.

'In doing so he unconsciously acts against himself, seeking to manipulate and control outcomes according to his own rules. He has forgotten that everything that is to happen for his benefit does so at the right time; and everything that is forced beyond a natural course of events is either lost or distorted. Even if the outcome is seemingly right it does not carry the power it would have had, or bring the benefit it was intended to bring. The result is that the harder he seems to push towards that which he wants, the further it moves away from him. Such is the plight of all who take the heritage of how they came to be for granted. Yet, in truth, knowing how to harness our natural synchronicity with life's opportunities creates the paradox that the less we do, the more we achieve.'

'So what can we do to regain this power, this heritage?' asked the pupil.

'We must steadfastly resolve to live, trust, accept and have purpose in whatever we do, at the moment we are doing it. For the nature of being always in the right place at the right time is ours to command.'

Resolving to change something in our lives requires us to let go of something. Yet, in so doing, we gain considerably more. A steadfast resolve does not mean making those frequent shallow resolutions we often indulge in, for they soon flounder and drown as soon as familiar old habits regain command over our intent. True resolve is both rare and sincere and is only made more profound by being tested in the worst circumstances over a period of time. Regardless of the duration of the period, it is, upon reflection, always timely, and provides the opportunity to express our stronger, truer self.

Our resolve is the measure of our commitment to that which we *know* is important to us. Without knowledge of our own unique what, why and wherefore, earnest resolve is neither forthcoming, nor will it endure when the obstacles inevitably encountered become too great. Consequently, when we seek security from something outside of ourselves, we join the rollercoaster of life; one which promises excitement when things go right, but also the risk of significant lows when they don't. Whenever we allow others control over the start and stop buttons of our life this further develops the false sense of self first spawned through our formative years. This leads to false desires and subsequently false activities, and, in turn, to false problems and false sufferings. The result is that we are continually out of sync with our true selves.

Regaining our natural synchronicity in the order of things is vital to every area of our lives. Whatever our situation or circumstance, it is where our current level of thinking has placed us. Quite simply, our thinking has manifested what our sense of self deems appropriate. It follows, therefore, that a true or false sense of self will align us with the opportune or inopportune, accordingly the infinite or finite. At birth we were fine, then well-meaning others unwittingly sought to *de*fine us for the best. It is now important to *re*fine ourselves in order to harness the abundance and opportunity specifically awaiting us. To re-learn the secret of being in the right place at the right time requires understanding and application of the following practices.

Living in the Moment

'Let us recall the tale of Chen Su-Lee, the famous turtle catcher,' said Wei Tzu, 'who ended up being caught himself. It was at a time when he was enjoying a lazy swim in familiar waters after a long and successful day's fishing. Suddenly he intuitively became aware of something following him. Turning, he saw what he knew to be a lethal giant eel and immediately sought to escape.

'Despite his strong strokes, his resourceful heart began to despair, for he knew that the water ahead held strong currents and his strength was depleting. With adrenaline coursing rapidly through his veins, he was able to reach a small rock in the nick of time. Resting just above the surface it would provide safety from the deadly eel. Safe at last he thought! Quickly he scrambled upon it and lay flat and still. He had only been there for a matter of moments when the awful realisation came to him that he was sharing his sanctuary with a sleeping venomous water viper. One bite from its evil mouth would bring his death instantaneously. No matter, thought the catcher, I will stay here until that monster eel has gone, and hope this viper continues its dreams. But, hearing a screeching noise above him, he looked up to see two gulls swooping down to land upon his resting place. His impending doom seemed certain, as already the viper had become aware of the disturbance. At that moment he noticed a half-open oyster shell and, ignoring his imminent fate, he plucked the most magnificent white pearl from within it and enjoyed its splendid beauty as it sat in the palm of his hand.

'You see,' concluded Wei Tzu, 'there was little point in feeling unhappy about how he happened to be in this situation. A catcher for most of his life, he had used all his experience to escape, so why waste his precious last few moments fretting over the future? Admittedly he had not taken the usual care recently, but what was past was history and all the hoping in the world would not change previous actions. The present moment, the very here and now, is the time to experience and cherish the fullness of what life offers. That is all any of us have at any one time. That moment must have our full attention.'

✲   ✲   ✲

When our life is supremely concentrated in the present, there is no need to worry about what has been, or be fearful about what may be. For the right response will come to us for every situation as it occurs. That is our real freedom; the ability to enjoy the choices we make in every successive moment of the present.

Very few people are able to live in the present moment of their lives. Whether in relationships or business, they allow their lives to be directed by past or future influences. Most choices are made under the rational mind that prompts, 'bearing in mind the circumstances, this is the most appropriate decision.' By letting go of all influences we are able to feel intuitively which direction we want to take, regardless of the circumstances.

Man-Ho Ping was a great but unhappy merchant. Leader of a group of businesses trading in sixteen provinces, he employed 10,000 people. Over the years the culture of his business had radically changed from one of harmony to one of defence and blame. On a rare visit to a local tea emporium he found himself next to his old friend Honest Lo.

'You look well old friend,' he declared in delight.

'But I cannot say the same of you Merchant Ping,' replied Honest Lo. 'For my eyes see a weariness and concern.'

'Indeed, I admit your eyes are correct. I believe that my ability to delegate has been the reason for my success, but the select team I have chosen to diligently train over the years are not performing as I had hoped. They have become focused only on results, which is what I had wanted, so that I could measure my growth. But the atmosphere is so tense when I am around them. What has happened? What should I do? These are the questions that give me my present expression.'

'Ah,' pondered Lo. 'In my experience of business and relationships, indeed any situation where there is interaction of thought, I believe that silence communicates more. Where is the usefulness of the pot, the external features or the emptiness inside? More is communicated by the empty space circled by

a group of people than is actually spoken from the circle. The emptiness tells you how things are.'

'Well the emptiness is not good,' agreed Ping. 'But how do I change it?'

'In training your team to become focused on results, you have moved away from the natural course of the way things operate. For though a river seeks to meet the ocean, it has no control over when. And though it is the nature of the acorn to grow, it has no control as to whether it will be successful. Power only exists over process, not results. So in delegating responsibility, one must also give the power to go with it. Having your people work on the process gives them the power needed to fill the emptiness of their former responsibility.'

With the focus of attention on results, the influence over process becomes weak. Systems break down and energy is then directed towards damage limitation through defence and blame.

In the early days of a business, the focus is clearly on the strengths that participants are able to bring to it. When these strengths are channelled into the daily process of what is best for growth, benefits in the form of increased productivity naturally result. This is similar to water in a river. Through its flow of focus and energy, it persistently seeks the path of least resistance rather than the shortest route. Consistently increasing in strength and substance, it always reaches its objective, the ocean, which, in turn, replenishes the river's source.

Once a business has matured, however, it seems to realign its focus of attention from strengths to weaknesses. It becomes like an enclosed canal, seeking to shore up weak banks which distract it from the shortest route required to maintain growth. Containing and protecting its position like a huge dam, it inevitably loses its fluidity. If the incoming river of new ideas and energy dries up, what does it matter when it has already contained a reservoir of resources? Yet water that is no longer fluid becomes stagnant.

Too many organisations, particularly larger ones, unwittingly illustrate, to their detriment, a reservoir culture. When natural flow is impeded, making headway becomes harder and the timing of opportunities is lost. Customers who rely on a service, for example, will soon form an opinion as to the culture of a company.

No-one has control over the results in their life. On first encounter this precept is understandably almost impossible to accept. The practice of manipulating the future forms the basis of most strategies in our modern world. This is coupled with the practice of planning a future on an expected outcome, rather than being one hundred percent aware of what is happening right where you are — the very here and now.

The man wanting to date a woman he really likes, for example, does not live in the present moment. First he is thinking of what she will say when he asks her for a date. Should her answer be yes, much of his 'here and now' is occupied planning the future event. Thoughts of the actual date occupy the days leading up to it. Thoughts of what may happen after dinner occupy the time spent eating dinner. Each present moment experience is lost as the mind is anticipating the future. If at the moment of the date unforeseen circumstances cause her to change her mind, the man has missed out on much more than an event. He has missed the experience of all those moments leading up to the date. If, on the other hand, the date goes ahead but does not conclude as anticipated, the man may then dwell in the past by analysing it.

We are only able to influence a result by what we do in the present, because the process of our lives is only contained within our present. We therefore have control over our processes, but we do not have control over our results. Although it is wise to establish the basis of an outcome, it is important to have flexibility in our thinking in order to anticipate and plan.

As we do not live in the future, we have no control over it. The majority of businesses, however, seek to make the future happen according to their wishes. The paradox is that the harder they push in an area they do not control, the more their desired result eludes them. By focusing one hundred percent of their energy on what is fully under their control, the process of what they do from moment to moment, they gain the greatest influence possible over a desired outcome.

When owners, shareholders and decision-makers who form the 'top line' of a company, are bottom-line driven, they become result-focused in their actions, rather than process-focused. In doing so they unwittingly put into motion those forces that actually bring about the reverse of that which they intended. Furthermore, when anticipated results do not materialise, focus is switched from the future to what is now a *past* process.

It is energy that makes things happen, and in this instance the term 'focus' refers to the level of energy. Physical form represents an outcome of energy transference; whatever is materially created must first be mentally generated. The quality of what we do, therefore, is dependent on the level of energy we are able to focus with. For example, in physics, it takes the same amount of energy to light a bulb as it does to cut with a laser, the latter is simply more focused. Metaphysically, whenever our energy is diluted, by thinking about what must happen, or what should have happened, to fulfil a result, we divert our energy away from the actual process that occupies our present. Yet it is our focusing on the present process that is the key to creating the results we desire.

Seeking control over a result requires us to interfere with

the process. A bird learns to fly through trial and error. With the care and attention bestowed from the parent solely focused on the process, the desired result comes about.

Merchant Man-Ho Ping had not let go of his 'young'. He had trained his team to fly, while at the same time clipping their wings. This prevented them from putting their hearts into flying, and instead focused their energy on vying for position within the nest. Business executives who seek to control results according to the way they believe things should be, unwittingly move the company's energy, and the energy of those they influence, away from present process into future results. Thus, the 'bird' whose clipped wings prevent further growth will ensure that its own position in the nest is kept by adopting a 'defend and blame' stance.

Living in the present requires us to focus on what we are actually experiencing, rather than what we hope to experience. Understanding fully that we only have control over process and not result, leads to the requirement and application of the next practice.

Trusting in the Moment

A man travelling with a convoy of traders between provinces was greatly concerned at the talk of bandits. Spying a distinguished gentleman in a great tent some distance from the convoy, he approached and said, 'Your pardon sir, but may I trust you with my purse?' Having received the gentleman's undertaking and promise to take care of the purse, the man returned to the convoy greatly relieved. But he immediately discovered that a band of thieves had robbed all the other traders during his absence.

Thanking his ancestors for his foresight, he hurried back to the gentleman's great tent to collect his purse. But he was shocked to see that the very same person with whom he had entrusted his purse, was distributing his fellow traders' belongings amongst the band of thieves. It was the robber baron himself.

'What have I done?' said the man. 'I have placed my wealth in the very same hand that I sought to keep it from! Who can be more foolish than me?'

As he retreated in fear, the robber baron noticed him and called out, 'You there, what are you doing?'

Shaken, the man replied, 'I came here to retrieve my purse, but alas, I discover that I have placed it in the very hands from which I wanted to keep it away.'

Looking at him intently the robber baron said, 'Please allay whatever fears you understandably have. For in truth, you are a man who put your trust in me. How can there be any question of me robbing you when you display such qualities? I gave you my word didn't I? So how can you expect me to keep your purse? Here, I now return it.'

This mutual act of trust and trustworthiness surprised some of the horde, but their leader's actions impressed many of them. It is said that in his later days Robber Baron became a great teacher.

By distrusting people we perhaps avoid a little loss, but the distrust that we sow in our hearts is a greater loss still. Only trustworthiness begets trust. Even when it does not, it still wins. In a materially driven world, in which a postage stamp is valued more than a word of honour because the stamp is sure, the argument is clear: 'Of course I would like to trust people, but people are not worthy of trust.' Although trusting others will inevitably mean that you must be ready to undergo loss, it is important not to look at the world this way.

It is not foolish to trust another, rather it is the wise person who trusts more than the foolish one. It is a greater strength to trust, for one who has less trust is weak and every day becomes weaker. One who does not trust others will find it difficult to trust even their own family and friends, and this distrust can develop to such an extent that they do not trust themselves. This is indeed sad, for the absence of self-trust is the basis of insecurity and lack of belief in one's self.

If you saw a man drowning would you shout, 'I would like to save you, but I do not know you well enough to trust you yet. You might pull me down with you'? The man certainly would not shout, 'Please get someone I can trust to save me.' He is trusting in you at that moment; a moment of complete trust that both you and he will afterwards always cherish. Trusting another is testing because there is the risk of loss. Whenever another places so much trust in us, we understandably re-evaluate the meaning of trust. When someone sincerely looks to us to be trustworthy, their very intent begins to develop trust within us, where formerly there may have been an absence of trust.

There is the argument, of course, that it is different in business. Were we simply to trust everyone we would most certainly lose everything. With every relationship, trust must first build, is the cry. It is because of this thinking that the basic role of trust must be understood.

Trust forms the foundation of every relationship, regardless of the situation or circumstance. Trust, similar to love, can be given but not necessarily received. The first person to give your trust to, therefore, is yourself. The immediate difficulty here is which you are you. When you realise the truism that your life unfolds in the way it does because 'wherever you go, you meet yourself', then you begin to consider how you can know which of your selves is the true one.

All the great teachers have recorded that man holds false ideas about himself. Certainly it would seem that if we changed the way we thought about ourselves, we would perhaps not have the problems we think we have. The reality is that 'knowing yourself' is easier said than done, so trusting yourself can be impossible. If you trusted yourself, however, there would be no need for second thoughts, which only serve to confuse issues. Perhaps if we experienced second thoughts first, many of our obstacles would diminish or disappear altogether.

As most of our problems spring from a lack of self-trust, rather than asking, 'What can I do about this problem?', we must learn to ask, 'What can I do to help myself?' The key to building self-trust is to go about it in the opposite way to that in which you have been taught to deal with problems. Whenever you experience a crisis, for example, take it completely on your own shoulders. Trying to share it with others immediately, in the belief that a problem shared is a problem halved, will have an adverse effect.

In diluting the intensity of the problem by sharing it around, you also dilute your power for understanding and removing it. The habit of discussing our problems, whether regarding finances, human relationships, or what we *should do* in life, stems from not trusting and heeding our own instructive advice. When you trust in your inner guidance you rise above your problem and the answer always comes to you at the right time.

Whenever you have a problem, look deeply into it. Its root will require a change in you which will in turn dissolve many other difficulties. A difficult marriage is not the issue, rather it is a false understanding of life itself and what you want from it. Difficult politics at work are not the issue, rather it is how greatly you believe that control, security, status and expectations have been compromised by the people involved. Frustration occurs when one's internal demands meet external opposition. In not getting what you want your desire turns back on itself, causing you conflict. It is a false sense of self which causes these desires, for it frantically believes that its existence depends upon their fulfilment.

The next time you allow yourself to experience the discomfort of what to you is a problematic situation, approach it differently. First of all, observe how your mind anxiously seeks for an answer, for relief and reassurance. Next, ask yourself if you really need the kind of answer you assume you do. Then let go of the problem's hold over you in the knowledge that you already carry the best solution within you. Finally, trust in yourself by *expecting* the solution at the right time to resolve the problem. In this way you will unconsciously gravitate towards the solution and recognise it as such when it comes to light.

Do not employ your memory to solve any inner problem that arises because of the manner in which you are addressing your external problem. Every moment of life is completely new and requires current insight. In the same way that you cannot make fire from stirring ashes, when you allow memorised action to leap into the space reserved for present consciousness, your creativity is blocked. Just try remaining quiet as you consider your next problem and see what happens. The answer may indeed come from a source outside of yourself, but you will recognise it as it will confirm what you already unconsciously know in your heart to be right.

Knowing when you have started to trust yourself will be discussed further, as it is a vital factor in developing intuitive business acumen. For now, accept the idea that trusting in the moment gives you great power. This must not be misunderstood as the fatalistic view of 'what will be, will be'. Far from it. Think of it instead as 'what you are, will be'. The degree to which you learn to trust yourself and your decisions is in direct proportion to the benefits you will reap at any moment. Trusting in the moment leads to the next practice.

Acceptance of the Moment

A female member of the disgraced Ling family went to visit the Old House of Ling, now under the direction of the Counsellor and Empress Ni. The house was formerly under the direction of the tyrannical Prince Ling, infamous for his mercilessly critical eye. His habit of seeing the flaw in everything and everyone led to fierce rebellion in his province, resulting in the stripping of his power.

Empress Ni was herself known as a woman of delicacy and compassion. On seeing the emaciated and ragged Princess Ling at her gate, she asked her to come in and prepared to give her words of comfort and such presents as would relieve her evident want.

But no sooner had the impoverished Princess said, 'I am a daughter of the family of Ling . . .' than the Empress forgot all about her charity. Her intent altered because of what she now saw before her and she shouted: 'A woman of the accursed Ling! You have come no doubt to beg for alms, forgetting what oppression your menfolk and their criticism caused to our family, how regardless of what we did we were treated without mercy, never being allowed any recourse . . .'

'No,' said Princess Ling, 'I did not come for sympathy, forgiveness or money. I came to see whether the family of Ni had learned from their ruthless predecessors, or whether the conduct you deplore was a contagion which would certainly end in the downfall of those who contract it.'

Empress Ni allowed her natural charitable emotions to be swept aside because of emotions belonging to, and residing in, the past. In losing her present compassion in favour of past grievances, she relinquished her power over her present and future actions. By accepting the past in favour of the present, she reacted in a manner that was supposedly alien to her natural character.

Often a parent is horrified to hear themselves criticising their offspring using the same admonitions they experienced so humiliatingly as a child. Many a rising executive gaining a higher position may employ criticism previously applied to his own efforts during his time as a subordinate. Both have accepted past experiences over the present. Both may be unconsciously prompted, through their conditioned thinking, by the misconception that the best support is through what is termed 'constructive criticism'. Experiencing the present moment, however, involves growing from the past, not imitating it. Feeling nervous, cynical or hard done by, for example, is caused by permitting past experiences to impose themselves upon the present moment. Yet the claim of the past upon the present is invalid.

Cynicism itself, that eternal impediment to growth, is commonly wrapped up in the guise of constructive criticism. When the habit of seeking and pointing out the flaw in something, whether in opportunities, arguments, presentations or behaviour, becomes endemic, the natural process is disturbed. The process of creativity, for example, is impeded when ideas being generated in a brain-storming session are evaluated at the same time.

A foible unique to mankind and born of lack of trust, cynicism prevents acceptance of process more than any other single factor. Whereas intuition stems from the facts presently at hand, cynicism relies solely on the past for its argument. Rather than seek the truth for itself, it demands to be convinced. The acceptance of present thinking should therefore involve encouragement. As true commitment is impossible without involvement, by encouraging the cynic to become more involved in a process rather than resisting it, he or she is allowed to embark upon the process that may result in them becoming a valued supporter.

Acceptance of the moment requires acknowledgement that each of us experiences a variety of rising and descending cycles.

In the same way that there is a time to sow and a time to reap, a time to consolidate and a time to grow, sometimes you do well in life and other times you do not. Evidently you enjoy life more during a high cycle and do not savour the difficulties characterised by a low cycle. The key is not to become excited by the high points, or depressed by the low points. In fact, the low points are to be respected because the high is built from the low. The *somebody* within you is built on the moments when you are *nobody*.

Generally we are not taught to value the low. We are conditioned to look for high respect and exaltation. When people have a low cycle they are emotionally debilitated by it, feel terrible and experience low self-esteem. Yet it is during these times, when they receive no attention or respect and do not love themselves, that they become wise and begin to grow. Princess Ling's character had strengthened to a point higher than Empress Ni's reputed one. Low signs, such as those we experience when nothing seems to be going our way, must be accepted as indications that we should pull back, reassess our situation, and perhaps consolidate in anticipation of the forthcoming growth cycle.

During its hot cycle, nature invests abundantly in the growth that follows its cold cycle. The old is discarded and, after a consolidation period, the new arrives. Nature accepts that you cannot grow without letting go. This natural cycle does not rest comfortably with individuals or business. The rare business wisely invests more than it spends in the high cycle in order that it can consolidate in a low cycle, however the ordinary business will not. In good times an organisation will show the market how wonderful it is through its large budget. In difficult times, when it is important for the market to know about them, the same organisation will be forced to keep quiet by its vastly reduced budget.

Although there is not one person or business that does not experience high and low cycles, only a fraction of both make provision. This is one of the reasons why the majority of businesses do not survive and why so many people suffer hardship during the influence of a major economic cycle. Preparing for the future during the present must not be confused with having one's consciousness in the future through worry.

No-one can avoid bad cycles either in health, wealth or relationships. But if we act in the same manner as if it were a good cycle, we will reduce our discomfort. This requires us to exercise the highest performance and highest service to ourselves and those around us. Accepting the moment irrespective of its influence requires the flexibility of the reed in the wind. It bends, then grows; it does not break.

Acceptance of the moment means accepting that what is presently happening may be an indication of something we have to change. For example, a man worrying over money may actually be worrying over being labelled a loser in society's money game. When he lets go of his false beliefs, the problem disappears. Perhaps the man's problem is being in debt through over-spending. Paying off his debts will not remove his compulsion to acquire objects in order to feel more secure.

When meeting any difficulty you must ask yourself, 'Am I going to fight this or rise above it?' If you decide to fight you will do so endlessly, for it is the very battling with the problem that keeps it going. Rise above it through using your own insight as to why you have this difficulty at the time that you do, and the problem disappears permanently. It does so because you realise that there wasn't an individual and a problem, there was only you, the individual, who *was* the problem. The moment you agree to solve yourself, you solve your problem. In doing this you begin to place yourself where you are intended to be. This brings us to the next and most important practice.

Purpose of the Moment

'There is plenty of time for that, when I have made my fortune. Everyone is always telling me that I have my whole life ahead of me, after all, and even you, Master, have always taught me that it's my life!'

'And so it is,' replied the sage. 'And your first duty must be to express yourself in your own unique way by being yourself. But to do that you must seek to harness your life force to the full, and that cannot be achieved without knowledge of your unique purpose.'

'I do hear what you say and I respect your wisdom, but try as I might I have no answer to that which I am do to. I cannot waste my life waiting to know what it could be. I'm going to seek my fortune first so I can then live my life to the full. Come with me and we'll both seek our fortunes together.'

'Now is my time for knowledge,' replied the sage, and watched as student Cheng marched off into the distance. It was some ten years before they met again.

'How so,' shouted Cheng, 'what brings a revered sage so far from home?'

'Now it is my time for life so I am travelling and teaching for a while. What fortune shines on you?'

'I have good employment,' Cheng replied, 'and a wife with three little ones, although they are not with me. But soon things will be different, it's just a matter of time.'

Ten years later Cheng met his former tutor at the Dragon Festival.

'Another world we meet, what brings you to this province?' Cheng asked. 'For my part I am very close to something important.'

'Now is my time for power,' replied the Grand Master. 'This province has been given to me to rule over for a while.'

'But you are a seeker of knowledge and a teacher, this is so different to what you have always done,' said the startled Cheng.

'Not so at all. It is the next stepping stone in the river of my life's purpose. My attention has been on one stone at a time, not on the river *flowing by. That I cannot stop and would not want to for it is the bringer of the opportunities that allow me to express my purpose. I follow each of my inclinations at a time, being assured of the stability of each stone before proceeding. In this way my direction is certain.'*

A further ten years and the two met while both meditating in the Garden of Contemplation.

'You look well, Old Master,' said Cheng. 'The years have served you better than the ones that have served me in this life. My life seems empty with lack of meaning. I have come here to pray for direction.'

'Now is my time for contentment and peace, and it warms my heart to see you again,' answered the old sage. 'Prior to this my time has served me well in respect of happiness of the heart. My initial inclination for knowledge put me in the right direction and every moment of my life I have sought to be ready to follow future inclinations at the right time.'

'It would seem that when a man intently and moment by moment is working on fulfilling his potential, he is expressing his purpose,' replied Cheng. 'The difference between us would appear to be that while I wanted to live my life to the full, you were doing so. What I believed was a future event was not at all.'

'Just so,' said the old sage, 'but even now we have a purpose to fulfil, because our rivers are still flowing. New water is as refreshing as when Youth meets Experience. It can never be too late to fulfil your purpose. It is a matter of letting go of what you believe is your security. For there is no security, there are only opportunities. Follow your heart and they will come to you.'

Every living being has a purpose, and it is the knowledge of that purpose that allows us to manifest the opportunities in the right place at the right time. Conversely, without knowledge of our specific purpose many of these opportunities will go unnoticed.

In our modern world fortunes are regularly spent on changing and improving methodologies, yet the majority of businesses continue to last less than one generation, and the majority of working people retire disillusioned and unfulfilled. Usually their enormous energy and potential is misdirected. Having an external objective is not the same as living a purpose that is internally driven.

Striving is futile if those energies available for our growth are working against us. As the proverb wisely goes, that is like running faster down the wrong road. When we are uncertain of our purpose we will be unable to recognise the direction that is right for us. Moreover, there can be no control over our destination if we are unable to recognise it for what it is when we arrive. When we are not in command of our own direction we will be distracted and go elsewhere. Our directions and arrivals relate to the processes and results we experience in our lives, and we *only* have the ability to control the processes. Once again, although the way in which we control our processes may ultimately influence our outcome, we do *not* have control over our results.

Whatever our purpose, it can be understood by studying the five inclinations everyone has hidden within the depths of their heart. Being absorbed in the way of the world, many do not take the time to decide what their purpose is, but at the same time there is a continual inclination towards it. These inclinations are as follows.

Desire of knowledge

Every child wants to know the reason 'why?' In time, the adult comes to believe, however, that work to earn one's bread and butter is the natural successor to education. We learn to get by and later strive in our work to get on until, without ever a moment to gain it, the hunger for knowledge is gone and the mind becomes blunted. Others, who do have time, tend to seek novelty. They think that to learn means to get to know something new.

Few of these will see that in every idea, however simple, is a revelation which will teach them more and more when they put their minds to it. Continuing to gain knowledge of what you are about, by understanding yourself and what motivates you, should be a part of daily life. In this way you are attracted to what is right for you to do.

Love of Life

This is as important to human beings as it is to every little insect that tries to escape your touch. However difficult and unhappy their life, every being wishes to live. Perhaps in the sadness of the moment a person might choose to commit suicide, but if he or she were in their normal state of mind they would not think of leaving the world. Not necessarily because the world is dear to them, but because their natural inclination is to survive.

Gaining of Power

In any situation power is sought because nature seems to sweep away anything that has no strength. The mistake we make is in the areas we choose to seek our strength. Power and control gained outside of ourselves over people and things can only remain limited. History illustrates how even the most powerful nations, built over hundreds of years, can be crushed in a very short time; individuals who seem to be all-powerful can be brought to their knees in an unforeseen moment. The real power we should seek is power over ourself.

Pursuit of Happiness

This is at the very heart of Man, although he seldom looks for it there. It is sought in leisure and pleasure, anything that will bring momentary happiness. The reality is that only virtue can bring real happiness. Anything that is transitory or which ultimately leads to unhappiness cannot be true happiness. Goodness leads to happiness. What is good *is* good, because it gives happiness, and if it does not do so it cannot be good, or right, or of virtue. Whenever Man has found virtue in unhappiness he has been mistaken; whenever he was wrong he was unhappy. Happiness is the very being of mind, and at any one moment Man knows how to question any source of unhappiness, though seldom seeks the answer of himself.

Attainment of Peace

You do not attain peace through rest, comfort or solitude. It is an art which is brought about when who we are and what we do is in harmony with our true self. It is natural to experience peace, but life in our world is far from peaceful. Animals and birds experience peace, but Man is the robber of his own peace. From seeking security outside of ourselves, either through constant acquisition, our position, or the stance we adopt, to our continual comparison with how successful we consider ourselves to be over others, rather than seeking self-reliance and co-operation, we have created an artificial life far removed from that which nature intended for us. The art of discovering peace is not in making outside conditions better for us; it is in seeking it within ourselves.

At some stage in their life everyone asks themselves: 'Why am I here and what am I to accomplish in life?' It is a fact that however discontented and restless someone may be, the moment they have purpose to their life a light goes on inside them. They may not be able to accomplish it but knowing it is there provides all the inspiration, strength, hope and vigour they need to pursue it.

One person with purpose will have greater power than a hundred working dawn 'til dusk not knowing their purpose. Out of one hundred people, ninety-nine will be discontented with the work they are doing. Either it is their life's condition that has placed them there, or it is because they have to work to live, or because they believe that they need to acquire the things that working makes affordable. By the time they have gathered what they need, the desire of wanting it has gone.

Having purpose determines our sense of right or wrong, good or bad. For example, one person whose vocation is to write plays and another whose vocation is to practise medicine, have their examinations before them. There is a play advertised which prompts them both to feel, 'I want to go and see it.' The medical student thinks, 'I should really study, but this is a good play and I must see it.' The playwright thinks, 'To go and see this play might be beneficial.' Both act in the same way, both see the same play, but one loses the sense of study and the other is inspired.

If we do not know what part we are to play in the symphony of life, we will not be able to produce the music that is so necessary for our personal satisfaction. When we are out of rhythm with the notes available to us, it is difficult to get back in tune.

What Have We Done Today?

Living, trusting, accepting and being in harmony with our purpose are the keys for ensuring we are in the right place at the right time. The secret is *knowing* that the application of these keys work. The sea turtle will carry her eggs, once fertilised, for up to four years, knowing that the time will come when she arrives at the right place to lay them. How many of her offspring will survive is still beyond her control, however.

When Man thinks only about what he wants to achieve at a later date, he fails to live his purpose from moment to moment. Like the turtle, many of us may carry our fertilised ideas and potential around for years, waiting for the right time and place to hatch them. The trouble is that the inner shell we have built up over our life prevents us from recognising when and where that time and place is. We either convince ourselves that we have missed out already, or that we can do whatever it is at some time in the future. It is vitally important that each of us begins to believe in ourselves.

Using our present effectively, becoming conscious of knowing what is right for us and what we are about, builds that belief. If we let go of debilitating ties to the past, such as grievances and failures, and cease to feel concern as to what may or may not happen to us, we allow all our energy to focus on positioning us in the right place at the right time.

> *We shall do so much in the years to come,*
> *but what have we done today?*
> *We shall give our gold in a princely sum,*
> *but what did we give today?*
> *We shall lift the heart and dry the tear,*
> *We shall plant a hope in the place of fear,*

We shall speak the words of love and cheer,
but what did we give today?

We shall be so kind in the afterwhile,
but what have we been today?
We shall bring each lonely life a smile,
but what have we brought today?
We shall give to truth a grander birth,
and to steadfast faith a deeper worth,
We shall feed the hungering souls of earth,
but whom have we fed today?

We shall reap such joys in the by and by,
but what have we sown today?
We shall build us mansions in the sky,
but what have we built today?
'Tis sweet in idle dreams to bask,
but here and now do we do our task?
Yes, this is the thing our souls must ask,
'What have we done today?'

Anon

The Fourth Scroll: Stalking the Heron

The Secret of Receiving Immediate Results
Through Infinite Patience

Yan Kan was worried. 'If I don't catch this bird soon the Emperor will carve me into meat for his dogs,' he complained to his friend, Cai Tok.

'Yes, thanks to your impulsive outburst about being able to bring him one with no difficulty at all. What demon possessed you to suggest that a mate for his pet heron would bring him great luck?'

'Because I thought it would be a good way for quick advancement,' answered Yan. 'Please help me. Receiving the Emperor's reward for bringing peace to his dynasty will mean high rank for us both and everything that goes with it.'

It had been some time before when the Emperor had discovered an injured heron in his garden. After it had been nurtured back to health, he had kept it caged, refusing to free it with the argument, 'Herons are omens and now that I have protected it, it in turn will protect me from the ill luck that continually haunts me.' Much later the bird sickened and began to lose its feathers. When the Emperor exclaimed out loud as to whether there would ever be an end to his misfortunes, Yan Kan had spoken out with his remedy. For the past month he had repeatedly tried to catch another heron but to no avail.

'Because of your impatience for a quick result you use methods that won't work,' said Cai Tok. 'This fine creature has an intuitive awareness of *approaching danger. You must seek to catch it using the ways of the heron. Observe it. Look for where it rests, for it does not build nests like others, its detachment is its strength. See how it stands, as evenly balanced on one leg as on two, yet as still as stone. Watch how it patiently fishes, immovable while its prey, unaware, swim by. You must be like that.'*

After stealthily moving towards the peaceful marsh that his prey frequented, Yan Kan submerged himself in the soggy ground while his friend covered him with the surrounding reed foliage. He soon learned that keeping so still was excruciating, and he longed to move. The marsh bed was at least comfortable, he thought, but it was so cold. It was hours later, just when he could hardly bear his imposed prison any longer, that he at last caught sight of the bird. The heron was returning. Knowing he would only have one chance, and would have to be quick, he forced all his concentration on what he was to do.

Flying low with legs hanging down, as herons do, the bird did not even touch the ground. Like lightning, a strong hand shot from the harmless-looking reeds and tightly clasped its leg. The surprise attack had been so fast that the startled creature was in a sack before it knew what had befallen it.

The Emperor was delighted and immediately placed the captive with the other. 'There now, my heron, I have a mate for you. What Emperor would be so generous as that? Between you now, keep my ills at bay!'

Shivering more from rage than fear, the newly captured heron was surprised to see her forlorn cousin and launched a deluge of questions including, 'But it has been so long, why did you not escape?'

'That is easy to say,' her cousin replied, 'but another thing to do. I have been impatient to get out for what seems my whole life, but the opportunity has never fallen to hand. Regardless as to how much I squawk and struggle, these bars hold me.'

'It seems that you have been around humans too long for you have struggled in the wrong way. To be free we simply have to act naturally.'

The next day the Emperor noticed that both birds lay completely still and, as he jolted their cage to stir them, their lifeless bodies remained so.

'What further misfortune is this?' he shouted in horror. 'They must have infected each other with some ill that they independently carried.'

Opening the cage the Emperor ordered the two dead birds to be removed. Within moments of being laid on the ground both herons immediately took to the sky.

'You see,' said the heron to her cousin, 'patience liberates. I was trapped by patience and now we are free through it. Patience will always bring a quicker result than impatience.'

'But we might have been buried alive,' the cousin protested.

'Yes, you have been around humans too long,' answered the other.

Having Certainty

Herons are fortunate in their ability to be patient in fishing for what they want. For his part, Man is unique in placing time constraints on the results that he wants in life and, in so doing, becomes restless rather than still. It is of course far easier to be patient for something when the outcome of it is certain, because in certainty there is less room for anxiety.

There is a direct correlation between patience and certainty as there is between impatience and doubt. The more impatient you are for something to go the way you want, the more you begin to question whether it will. Say, for example, you begin to question an intuitive idea that you were once certain was right. Your questioning causes you increasingly to doubt it, until you think it is absurd and either ignore it or distort it to fit into your 'perfectly rational' constraints. Although the idea was most certainly right, your rationale, influenced by your impatience to get where you're going, perceives it as wrong, or at least too slow a route to your desired result.

The key to being patient, therefore, is in having greater certainty of the outcome. The immediate obstacle for us in accepting this, though, is how we can be certain of an outcome when we can only influence, not control, an event and time that has not yet happened.

This concept is alien enough to our conditioned thinking, but harnessing the immense power that infinite patience affords requires us to go further into previously forgotten ways of thinking. Yet in applying the prerequisites of the concept, one begins to recognise, or know again, that it is a *natural* way of thinking; a new unbounded way that produces quicker results, for without doubt patience with another reflects the measure of patience we have with ourselves. This is the basis of the paradox – only infinite patience produces immediate results.

Before understanding what is involved, stop reading for a moment and, thinking from your heart rather than your head, reflect on the truth of the following concepts, (1) Harnessing the power of infinite patience will put you at ease. (2) The absolute certainty that what you deeply want for yourself inevitably happens will free you from your insistence on having it now.

Your thoughts have no doubt re-affirmed what is seemingly common, or natural sense. But common sense is rarely common practice. What *is* common practice is allowing the ego's demands, based on fear and impatience, to dominate our thinking. It is the ego that insists on having what it wants now by convincing us how much is missing from our life. If its demands are not satisfied it convinces us how unfair life is. Conversely, if we do satisfy it, it will simply furnish us with another set of demands tomorrow. Freedom from the distracting ego is discussed in the seventh scroll, but right now, as long as we allow the ego to dominate our thinking, we will not attain the infinite patience that detachment from outcome requires.

Acknowledging Our Universality

We must seek to cultivate infinite patience through being certain about our outcomes, while simultaneously being unconcerned as to when and how. This involves understanding our relationships with everything around us. In the same way that a drop of water taken from the ocean has the characteristics of its source, so each of us are actually part of an Infinite Universal Spirit. Throughout the ages numerous cultures have referred to the Spiritual Force that dwells in everything.

In the West we refer to the Infinite Universal Spirit as God. Over the centuries fixed interpretations of God have conditioned us, either wittingly or unwittingly, to believe that this Infinite Loving Spirit is something actually apart from ourselves and indeed jealously sitting in wrathful judgement of us. Enlightenment, or the conscious self-realisation of our oneness with God's Universal Spirit, removes the limitations that are set through the belief that God is outside of us.

The New Testament refers to the *Kingdom of Heaven within;* the Holy Koran to *Those who know themselves, know their God;* the Upanishads, *To know God is to become God* and *by understanding the self, all this universe is known;* The Tao Teh Ching to *Know that what is, is in everything;* and many others appear in every spiritual work, all reminders of our connectedness with the Universal Oneness of God.

Irrespective of one's faith, or name, term or definition of God, as such a thing is very much a personal choice, acknowledging that you are part of a Universality that is infinite in its possibilities allows you to recognise that what you want cannot be kept from you. It follows that our ability to trust in this connectedness is proportionate to our ability to know that we will receive. This acceptance in turn allows us to remove all demands and time constraints as to how and when we will receive, thus cultivating the virtue of infinite patience. In harmony with other paradoxical truths, the very action of releasing the impeding forces that impatience and attachment unwittingly attract allows the more immediate realisation of what you want.

Take two individuals studying to become proficient in a particular subject. One is desperate to gain recognition of his proficiency and seeks either title, badge or award. The other, absolutely certain of the outcome of the dreams that originally motivated him to study, yet unconcerned as to how or when they will be fulfilled, receives recognition ahead of the first. While the first attached his feeling of importance to the award, the other had let go of his expectations and went about his daily business.

Letting go in the knowledge that you will receive is infinitely more powerful than holding on in the hope you may receive, as it places your energy in harmony with the order of the way things work. Admittedly this is a difficult concept to accept, as patiently detaching ourselves from those things which are important to us is in direct conflict with the way we have been taught.

Imagine someone with the following choices. The first choice is feeling happy only when things turn out just the way they want. The second choice is feeling happy whether things turn out the way they wanted or not. Although the obvious choice is the latter, in reality almost everyone adopts the former. The second choice can only be experienced through the practice of patient detachment.

Consider your involvement with a current situation that holds great importance to you. Think about when you want it to reach a fruitful conclusion. Take a moment to observe how you feel. Now, in the knowledge that you will continue to go about your business diligently, patiently detach yourself from the outcome. Observe how you feel now. Say to yourself that because you are absolutely certain that what you want will come to pass, you are completely unconcerned as to how or when it will. Observe how you feel now. Notice how, if what you were thinking of concerned you, your feelings of frustration and anxiety diminish. Notice also how, if what you were thinking of inspired you, a new certainty smothered rising doubts.

Although it is good to lose frustrations, doubts and anxieties, your ego begins to feel uncomfortable as its power over you is threatened. Knowing how to squeeze your Achilles heel, it immediately seeks to quell any rebellion by your true self by convincing you that such passive thinking will never gain you what you want. Your impatience is positive, the ego will suggest, as it fuels you to push for what you want and is therefore crucial for your security.

As these demands increase, your anxiety level increases. The ego does not want you to feel your connectedness with everything, for in allowing that, it removes its main source of power in making you feel unique. The less you feel singled out for what life offers, the harder the ego has to work to convince you that your security is under continual threat. If you become internally driven rather than externally influenced for your security needs, then the ego is out of a job.

Why Me?

'All my life I have been singled out!' the Emperor complained to Mai-Lee, his favourite concubine. *'The gods have their favourites and I have never been one of them. This Dynasty has been plagued with misfortune since I became Emperor, despite what I do. What ills did my ancestors perform for me to be treated so?'*

'But now that the blue heron is under your protection, my Lord, a new day will dawn,' consoled Mai-Lee.

'Just so, and in quick time too, or it will bode ill for him,' retorted the Emperor. *'I have told him that as Yan Kan has procured a mate for him so he must use his power to keep away further time-wasting misfortunes.'*

The Emperor thought about his five-year rule, in which he had sought to increase his wealth as quickly as possible to avoid future dangers. Didn't his people see that they must all pull together to fill his coffers so that he could protect them? That infernal Sage Ti-Ling Tzu had tried to advise him otherwise of course: *'There are three dangers in the world,'* he had said. *'To have many privileges but few virtues is the first danger. To be high in rank but low on ability is the second danger. To receive wealth without personally accomplishing much is the third danger. People may gain by loss and may lose by gain.'*

What impudence! A leader such as he was beyond such things. Putting him to death had been too good for him. Fancy being told that *'the way of rulers is to live frugally so that the citizens will not resent them.'* He liked to display his braids of importance. How would everyone respect him otherwise? He would be stronger than his predecessors whatever it took, and he would force it to be done in the shortest possible time. He longed for the day when he would be recognised as the most powerful ruler of his dynasty. His former sage had counselled that it would be wise to plan a consolidated growth. But that would take a generation! No, he would do it in one tenth of that time.

'My Lord,' cried Mai-Lee waking him from his reverie. *'There is a commotion at the aviary and the keeper begs your attendance!'*

The Emperor had been shocked to see his two herons take to the sky. *'I am being wrongly punished,'* he lamented. *'How can I assure myself of my rightful success when I am besieged by misfortune on all sides? Someone will pay for this unfairness! Where is Yan Kan?'*

Often when we decide we want something, we want it now, and when we do not get it straight away, we feel that life is unfair, that we have been treated unjustly, even cheated. Sometimes we convince ourselves that it is because others, and even forces beyond us, do not want us to have what we want. In choosing to believe that we have been singled out, we may rationalise that we must do unto others before they do unto us, or, at the very least, get in first before others, rather than adhere to the Golden Rule of treating others as we would wish to be treated. In taking things personally, we convince ourselves that the acquisition of our desires is at the mercy of the inquisition by others.

Every time we allow ourselves to become impatient, we are devaluing ourselves and failing to trust in the power of our connectedness with everything. In doing so we consider ourselves as separate from the Universal Intelligence we know as God, and assume that if things are not going the way we want, it is because we are being punished for previous misdeeds or are being singled out.

God is not the individual personality with mortal values that Man has created; the unconditional love that God has for us holds no judgements about one person being more entitled to abundance than another. Since God is everywhere in everything, there are no favourites. Punishing you by making all the traffic lights turn to red, or by refusing to grant you a single parking space when you are short of time, does not figure in God's great design. It is our own confused thoughts that attract the seemingly chaotic events we experience.

To view the realisation of what you want as a favour is to begin the process of bargaining with God, which most do more acutely when their needs must. Seeking to strike deals stems from believing that every individual is separate from other living beings. The Universal Spirit responds to you when you recognise it for what it is, a oneness of which you are very much a part. In recognising it, you are able to attract what you ardently want, and which already exists, to yourself.

Admittedly, this is not immediately digestible. Our daily actions of judging and evaluating others form a continuous stream of affirmations that render any understanding of our oneness with others impossible. Just because we are physically separate, however, it does not follow that we are metaphysically separate. Our bodies are not separate from the Universe which, metaphorically speaking, is our *extended* body; but our physical bodies simply allow us to experience the Universe through our intricate system of receivers and transmitters.

Each of us is like an individualised energy wave sending out and receiving thoughts which co-ordinate or tune in with matching vibrations. Being impatient, for example, will cause you to emit, and thus attract, a different level of vibration which, although it will match what you unconsciously asked for, is not what you actually wanted.

When you practise infinite patience towards an outcome, you literally transmit an *undistorted* wave of energy for your extended body to receive. Your extended body locates the existence of the objectivity that matches the subjectivity of your transmission, and manifests it for you. The result is quicker because the intention transmitted is infinitely clearer. Our extended body will not recognise our demands as to how and when it should deliver to us, it will only recognise the clarity of why we want to receive. Demanding that God delivers according to a particular timetable and format, reinforces the false idea of God as a disconnected force. There is only one power in the universe and you are connected to that power.

The level of consciousness required to manifest objects instantaneously is known as 'siddhi consciousness'. It is a level at which the period of pure thought, from transmission to reception, is instantaneous. Sri Sathya Sai Baba, who millions claim is the Avatar of our age, has attained this level of consciousness. Living in Puttaparthi, southern India, his manifestations have been witnessed and recorded by the most respected Western and Eastern professional institutions. One can only suppose that as this level requires complete faith in accepting that we are one with God without limitation, this would preclude any abuse of such immense power.

Although each of us holds the potential to attain such a level of consciousness, we have conditioned ourselves within our environment not to require it. What we are able to accomplish, however, are more immediate results simply through patience.

Experiencing this is by far the best way to see the results that it delivers. Over a seven-day period, make a list of everything that is important for you to achieve, either short term or long term. Focus particularly on those elements that, however small, seem to frustrate you — they literally try your patience. During this time become conscious of whenever you feel impatient or frustrated. Each time you feel these emotions remind yourself that you are entirely unconcerned as to when or how the object that is causing your impatience or frustration will come about, or be resolved. Just say to yourself that you are certain that whatever will happen will be in your best interests.

Persevere and you will be astounded at what will happen. Be aware of things that begin to show up in your life which you have not noticed before. Although they may not be quite what you're expecting, the frequency with which they appear will make you more conscious of them. Act on whatever you begin to notice, while trying very hard to release all judgement towards events. Trying to prejudge the result is a sure indication that you are once again becoming attached to the shape of life as it used to be.

The synchronistic happenings you are experiencing are resulting from a heightened consciousness prompted by your patient detachment. At this level you are now consciously making contact with the universal source of energy that was previously below your conscious level. Remember to act on the things that are now coming to you, as this signals to the universe that you are ready to receive. Whether or how you thank your connectedness to the Universal Spirit for sending you the people and events to fulfil the right outcome for you is, of course, a matter of individual choice.

The Instruction of Obstruction

'So his obsession with not letting go of anything finally caught up with him,' commented Yan Kan to himself, on hearing news that the Emperor had met with an untimely end.

It had been several years now since Yan Kan had fortuitously escaped the Emperor's wrath. It had been his experience of stalking the heron that had led him to see things in a different light. When water accumulates, it breeds predatory fish. And when rites and duties become decorations, they breed artificial and hypocritical people. The title and rank that the Emperor had quickly invented and thrown to him that day, and which he had so obsequiously caught, were now empty and meaningless to him.

He had decided at that moment to apply his new-found virtue of patience to more meaningful pursuits and departed the Court. He would no more attach such importance to false things. And he would no more suggest solutions that sought reward by pandering to the whims of another in authority. Any leader who demanded, needed or revelled in such bolstering was an insecure leader. How strange it is that when rulers have obsessions, their subjects do a lot of posturing; when a ruler is crafty, their subjects are devious; and when a ruler is demanding, their subjects are contentious. Any ruler who blamed ill luck for the state of his kingdom and sought to determine outcomes by using his strength to hold on to something weaker, was bound to fall sooner or later.

Yan Kan felt no surprise that the Emperor had lost his life through his rigid attachment to his policy for growth and recognition. His wise friend, Cai Tok, had been right: *'When political leaders ruin their countries and wreck their lands, themselves to die at others' hands, it is always because of their impatient desires.'*

Since becoming a merchant, Yan Kan had determined to himself that he *would follow the sage-like philosophy he now knew to be true: 'To be able to use the power of other people, it is necessary to win people's hearts. To be able to win people's hearts, it is necessary to have self-mastery. To be capable of self-mastery, it is necessary to have patience.'*

Yan Kan resolved to apply patience in everything, particularly when he encountered the obstacles which he had discovered were as much a part of business as they were of life. 'The ancients were certainly wise in creating writing symbols that contained the meanings of both crisis and opportunity. I will see every obstacle as a further reminder to be infinitely patient and unattached to any particular schedule. For in such flexibility lies the power to cultivate the hidden pearl of opportunity from the grit of adversity.'

To have the virtue of patience, it is important to acknowledge obstacles as opportunities to strengthen you, not as indications of failure. In attempting to patiently let go of an outcome, there will be a tendency to view obstacles that begin to appear as evidence that what you are embarking upon is not working. The ego will always use such obstacles as proof to deny the existence of your connectedness to a universal energy. In doing so it attempts to regain its influence over you, which your new actions of patience and detachment are causing it to lose.

Detaching yourself from an outcome does not mean giving up on it. Determination and persistence are valuable ingredients in both testing your resolve and surmounting life's inevitable obstacles. The message of this scroll must not be misinterpreted as an opportunity to just sit back and do nothing and everything will be taken care of. It is to continue to ensure that you go about your daily routines, relative to what you are working towards, while being unconcerned yet certain of outcome.

The art of receiving immediate results for yourself through infinite patience lies in occupying a higher state of awareness, rather than allowing yourself to feel that you are being pushed around by whims that are out of your control. Consider the difficulties that have caused you to re-evaluate your life in order to surmount them. Your reflection will no doubt confirm that each one was both timely and appropriate, although it did not seem so at the time.

Your reflection will no doubt also reveal to you that more patience would have surmounted the difficulty with less pain than your impatience gave you. However, when you are impatient to get out of something, or into something for that matter, you are more liable to compromise yourself. The fact is that every obstacle you encounter offers the opportunity to propel you to a higher state of awareness. It provides a test of your certainty of attaining what you have resolved to attain. There is no timetable when you have infinite patience and there can be no failure when you have detached yourself from how the desired result will come about.

Patience builds serenity.
Great people are serene, free from longing;
they are calm, free from worry.
Being calm and joyous, without pride,
one attains harmony.
Harmony is the essence of Oneness
from which immediate results derive.

The Fifth Scroll: Fighting the Rat

The Secret of Harnessing Your True Conscience Power

'What a terrible dream I experienced last night!' howled Gate-Keeper Yin to his wife. 'A giant rat would not desist from chasing after me until, finally, with no place to turn, it had me cornered.'

'Heaven protect us against such things! What did you do?' his spouse enquired earnestly.

'What could I do but attack it?' Yin continued. 'And I fought hard let me tell you, but in the end I was sorely wounded. But then a very strange thing happened. Just as I lay in a defeated crumpled heap of humiliation, expecting the final mortal blow, the rat spoke to me. It said: "You win," and immediately helped me up, which is when I awoke. What awful misfortune can it possibly foretell?'

'My old mother was wise,' answered his wife, seemingly calmer in her remembrance of something. 'She would say: "When you have a fight with your conscience and get beaten, you win!" Maybe that rat was your conscience and you've gone and cornered yourself.'

'How so?' asked Gate-Keeper Yin, and his thoughts immediately flew to his actions of the past week. With so many people arriving for the festival this year, he had allowed his greed to get the better of him. He had charged more, in the certainty that with so many travellers, he would not get caught

out. Some had looked perplexed at the toll cost, a few had made him feel a
cheat, but as most had simply paid up he had ignored the feeling which then
soon left him. Anyway, he reasoned, he deserved such perks!

'Don't ask me, I am no sage!' replied his wife. 'Though I would imagine
that any battle you lose with your conscience must mean you ultimately win.
Particularly if it causes you to stop doing something that will bring you no
good. Have you been up to no good?'

Conscience is that part of our consciousness that is vital to our
development and growth. However, there is conscience and
true conscience. The former is subjective, the latter objective.
We often think the function of our subjective, or *conditioned*,
conscience, is to spoil life for those of us who are unlucky
enough to be pricked by it. It could be said that 'your
conscience doesn't keep you from doing anything, it merely
keeps you from enjoying it.' In this guise it can be likened
to an irritating acquaintance that you have periodically to
tolerate. All too often we construct an entire framework of
intelligent rationa-lies-ations in our attempts to justify actions
that contradict our deepest sense of right and wrong.

Without understanding and development of our true conscience, that internal guide that provides clarity and guidance,
its valuable power will remain untapped. It will lie dormant
behind our conditioned conscience which asks: 'Will I be
found out?' If not we reason, then everything will be okay.
When true conscience is harnessed, however, we are able to
break down the internal barriers that prevent us from facing
our inner contradictions and see the truth about ourselves. In
doing so we are able to achieve a level of inner security that is
reflected in every area of our personal and professional lives.

There are numerous situations which, although seemingly
small and insignificant, we see as a normal and acceptable part
of our everyday behaviour, both personally and, in particular,

professionally. They will often appear as simply the *normal* way of doing business. We cheat on our taxes or expense account; we tell little white lies in our business dealings; we keep quiet when we are given too much change. Though we like to believe that our word is our bond, we change our minds about honouring agreements that we have made with others, hiding behind a man-made caveat. We exaggerate or omit information as we consider appropriate, in order to get what we want.

Conscience guides us as to what is good or bad concerning our conduct with others. Yet we have become adept in generating a rationalisation for every one of our small dishonest acts in order to justify them on a mental level. On a deeper level, however, as they remain unjustified and unresolved, they drain our sense of self-worth. Over time their amalgamated and compounded effect contributes to confusion, guilt, loneliness, ulcers, cancer and heart attacks, as our inner fears and conflicts attack our bodies.

Culture, Morality and Conscience

A difficulty in discriminating between our conditioned dis-empowering conscience and our true empowering conscience, is that what is seemingly right for one particular culture may be viewed as wrong by another. For example, one culture may choose to receive payment from the person accused of causing the death of a family member as appropriate compensation, but this custom of accepting 'blood money' could be considered immoral by another culture. Because of different cultural views, therefore, it is important to differentiate between morality and conscience.

Very simply, where morality is relative, always different and always changing, conscience is absolute and never changes. Morality can be both subjective and objective. Take the example of cheating another person, objectively accepted as wrong by Mankind, but too often subjectively acceptable between people of different classes, education and even countries.

Conditioned conscience comes from an association of ideas. Such an association can cause us to act in a particular way in order for us to feel comfortable about what we do. Although there may indeed exist, or have existed, those rare individuals who actually appear to be without conscience and do what they do for the sake of evil, the purpose of the conscience is to direct for the good. A person acting from conscience may cause destruction in the misguided belief that they are doing so in the interests of good, and this in itself illustrates the havoc a conditioned conscience can cause. Although history records various atrocities perpetrated by seemingly remorseless individuals, it also records that, without exception, what they unconscionably strove to create eventually crumbled.

External morality is different everywhere, as exemplified in the maxim, 'When in Rome, do as the Romans do.' For inner morality you must be able to *do*; that is do what you know to be true in the very depths of your heart. When developed to its stronger and deeper state, your true conscience becomes a powerful guiding tool of discrimination and direction.

People will always claim that if it weren't for your conscience, you'd probably do everything you want to do right away. In educating our conscience, however, we are able to align what we do with what we are. It also helps us to recognise that there are universal principles, independent of us, allowing us to understand the futility of trying to become a law unto ourselves.

Keys to Releasing Conscience Power

Dealing with those who do not appear to have a conscience can often create a rationale for not heeding our own. The truth is that as long as your conscience is your friend, you never have to worry about your enemies. However, the thought of responding differently from an habitual fear-based reaction may appear so frightening that it is almost unimaginable to us.

Could we really confront our boss or client? Could we really tell the truth or say what we think, even if it meant that the outcome was not the most financially desirable? Could we really live true to our conscience, even if it meant being fired or impeding our advancement? Could we really trust that we would be peacefully guided towards our next job, contract or opportunity, instead of remaining in a compromising situation or fearfully grasping at whatever becomes available to us? Whatever fears we feel corner us, it is not until we confront them that we will stop feeling compromised in a way that literally drains our energy and potential.

In harnessing our conscience we will be clearly guided towards balanced growth and development. There are three specific keys which when practised will release the power of true conscience, allowing it to become the ally and trusted advisor it is intended to be.

Motives over Moves

T'ien K'ai was a rich philanthropist whom everyone in the village liked. Whenever he himself received further good fortune he would share it by giving rice and money to the poor. One very poor man received a heavy sack of rice which he happily took home to his family. Upon emptying it into his storage bin, however, he discovered ten gold coins mixed in with the rice. His wife was delighted but the husband said, 'Lord T'ien K'ai gave me rice. He did not intend for me to have this gold. I must make him aware of his mistake by returning the gold to him.'

'Don't be such a fool!' his wife said. 'We are poor and he certainly won't

miss a few coins as he has immense wealth. Give them to me and I will go to the market and change them for money.'

They argued but the husband was adamant. 'We must not be greedy. I cannot take what is not intended for me. Anyway, it was I who brought the rice and the gold home in the first place.'

Returning to T'ien K'ai the following day he told him, 'You were so generous in giving me and my family such a large sack of food, but I have discovered these ten gold coins. I've come to return them as, although I am a beggar, I am not a scoundrel and can recognise a mistake when I see one.'

The rich philanthropist was moved by the poor man's sincerity and replied, 'I want you to keep them, and because of your sincerity, I will double their amount. You came with ten coins and you will leave with twenty and I give these to you now, personally, so that you will know there is no mistake.'

A greedy businessman happened to overhear the story and he came up with a brilliant idea. He visited the poor man and offered to exchange six of the gold coins for money. The poor man was happy to oblige. Then, putting on the clothes of a beggar, he went to visit the house of T'ien K'ai.

'I will do the same thing as the beggar and double my wealth,' he said to himself. 'With the hundreds of bags that have been received by beggars I will never be suspected as not being one of them.'

When his turn came for an audience with T'ien K'ai the disguised beggar said, 'Yesterday you gave me three coins but look! They have magically become six coins today. I have, therefore, returned to your house so that I can give back the original ones to you while I keep the other three.'

'Although one man brought back the same amount that I gave him,' replied T'ien K'ai, 'you are the only person to whom I have given, whose wealth has increased. I am delighted for you, but tell me, what can I do for you now?'

'It is said that you value honesty,' answered the businessman-beggar. 'If, because I am returning your coins you are impressed with my honesty, then perhaps you will reward me with more. After all, you would never have known the original three produced three more if I had not returned.'

'Yes,' said the philanthropist, 'you do deserve more. But since you have *already made six from three coins let me give you something much more important than just a few more.'*

'What reward do you have in mind?' enquired the excited business-man curiously.

T'ien K'ai summoned his first secretary and instructed him to write out a Certificate of Honesty. When it was completed T'ien K'ai attached it to the false beggar's back and signed it. 'There you are,' he told the businessman-beggar. 'This certificate will announce to the whole world that you are a most honest man. I have never awarded such an honesty document to anyone else. But you deserve it.'

The only way to gain and keep the goodwill and high esteem of the people we work and live with is to deserve it. Each of us will eventually be recognised for what we are because of our motives, not for what we try to be through our moves. Having the right motives will always win over making the right moves, yet, often prompted by personal ambition, we focus on gaining quick success by learning artful techniques. In the long run, no technique, no matter how clever, can conceal the motives a person has in his or her heart.

Many businesses focus on making all the right moves with the understandable motivation of greater return. Indeed, the majority of employment training is on specific competency techniques to ensure that the right moves are practised. But the motives behind practising the right moves are not always in harmony with what the business purports to be in business for.

Take two competing pharmaceutical organisations, for example. Both are giants in their industry, committed to providing essential cures for the greater enjoyment of life. One company may seek to maximise its returns so that it can invest in further research and development in order to keep its pipeline of essential cures flowing. Another may seek to maximise its returns so that it can bring a greater return for its shareholders. The first considers that developing new cures is its life blood and this is in line with its motives. The second considers that its shareholders' goodwill is its life blood.

Both companies are making the right moves. Yet do they both have the right motives? Without further development, what will the second company do for new products? It will need to effect the take-over of another pharmaceutical company in order to obtain further products. This may be the right move, but the consequential reduction of duplicated personnel will inevitably mean the disappearance of many people, ideas and research that would have led to new products.

At the other end of the scale are two small businesses. Both are specialists in their industry, committed to providing greater efficiency in the operations of their clients. The first seeks to sell its products and services in the belief that they will make a difference. As such this company is discerning and does not seek to sell its products if it believes they are inappropriate for the customer's requirements. This is in line with its motives. The other, however, is motivated to sell because its over-extended budget must be met. Regardless as to whether a product is appropriate or not, it believes that as long as the right moves are adhered to, success is assured. It is essential to focus on the right motives as then the right moves naturally follow.

To receive rewards through financial or career success by making the right moves, at the cost of high self-esteem and peace of mind, is to have sacrificed something of real value for mere trinkets. When we exchange gold for trinkets, the quantity we amass is irrelevant. Initially, and for a limited period, possessing the trinkets may be exhilarating, but you will not keep people from noticing the difference.

Walk into a building that houses any business that you are

not involved with, and you can soon tell whether its moves are consistent with its motives. Hidden agendas, dichotomy of values and duplicity of motives that have become 'the way it is around here' cannot be concealed for long from an outsider. The tension generated by inconsistent motives can permeate a whole company. Notice, for example, the tension we experience when trying to please people from whom we want something. As an individual you only have to ask yourself if you feel differently taking to someone that you want something from, than you do when talking to someone that you don't want anything from. When you are sure of your motives you believe in what you do and why you are doing it, then you can learn to become as relaxed with others as you are when by yourself. Questioning your motives on a regular basis will automatically develop the power of your true conscience. In doing this your conscience helps you to be sincere with yourself.

Although we are rarely aware of it, we always treat others exactly as we treat ourselves. So, if we are unsure of our own motives, it follows that we will be unsure of the motives of others. Understanding the motives of others accurately, however, would clearly be an immensely valuable tool, as all areas of our lives involve interaction with others. Understanding of the right motives is infinitely more important than simply acting out the right moves, and this leads to the application of the second key.

Facing the Fear of Honesty

'But, Father, how can I tell the teacher? Everyone will say that I ratted on Li-Li and hate me!'

Yu Kan looked at the despair in his son's eyes and his heart went out to him, while his mind recalled how his own schooldays had taught him to face the grim realities of battling with a misguided code of honour. 'You must ask yourself how you cannot,' he replied. 'This is no simple prank. If you saw that it was Li-Li who was the real culprit and say nothing, then everyone will have to take the blame.'

'Yes, but everyone is prepared to,' his son argued, adding quietly, 'because they are scared if they do not. Li-Li has said that if anyone tells then they are a coward and, as such, they will deserve to be punished by him.'

'Yet each time he gets away with his behaviour he seems to grow worse, from what you tell me. With everyone's silence clearly condoning his actions, no-one is helping him to question them.' Yu Kan paused. 'You must follow what your conscience tells you, for to know what is right and not to do it is as bad as doing the wrong yourself. It takes greater courage to do something that you feel you should do, than to not. The coward is the one who does nothing, when everything inside directs them to do something.'

'But why me?' said his son, looking horrified at what his father was implying. 'Why do I have to do anything? Why can't someone else?'

'Because only you can fight your own battles, and your own battles are the ones you feel strong enough about. The pain that you imagine lies ahead of you for doing the right thing will not be as great as the pain you will give to yourself for not doing so. You will not like yourself.' Again Yu Kan paused. 'So, there is your choice.'

'So, either I hate myself if I keep quiet, or everyone hates me if I speak out. Some choice!' answered his son.

'That's it,' said Yu Kan. 'But remember, real honour and respect comes from being your own man, not from being fearful of the whims of others.'

The following day the boy went to Li-Li and asked him to own up to what he had done. Li-Li refused and threatened a beating if the boy was to tell. The boy did tell, and the next day he sported his bruises proudly and, after a short time, became more popular than Li-Li, but for all the right reasons. After all, he had confronted and conquered his fear of being dishonest. He liked himself and he could live with himself. He was his own man.

* * *

The moral and ethical situations that we encounter in both our personal and professional lives are important opportunities for us to choose between fear and its opposite, love. Having the courage of your convictions stems from how much you like yourself. Before continuing, reflect on the following. On a percentage scale of one to one hundred, how much do you like yourself?

Identifying our fears is usually the easiest part; it is confronting them that is difficult. If we peel back the layers of our fears far enough, we will often discover that their main source lies in our belief that we feel we are not worthy or lovable. A form of 'honour amongst thieves' leads us to misguidedly believe that 'ratting' on the wrong actions of another is a crime. Speaking up for yourself is not about collaboration with the enemy. Tribal associations of 'not telling tales' follow us from school through to social and work dilemmas. In allowing the creation of such fears we directly affect our own self-worth. Indeed, the majority of abuses, physical, emotional or mental, remain unknown, or continue, because of prior conditioning to keep quiet about them.

Acceptance of intimidation at work, for example, can be observed everyday. A unanswered memo to a subordinate will be perceived by a 'bully' as acquiescence while, in truth, the recipient believes his or her silence indicates their non-acceptance. The arrival of internal e-mail permits blanket bullying of whole departments. Staff wanting to make a stand against something they do not agree with stay silent. Instead, they reserve their complaining for unofficial lines of communication such as the canteen or home; the grapevine shouts louder than official lines, yet remains unheeded.

As our fears have often been with us for a long time, we come to believe that we are not worthy of the respect, success, financial stability and peace of mind that we really would like. We perceive situations in a fearful way, based on indoctrinated beliefs such as the following:

(1) Sometimes you have to do things that are not entirely ethical because they are part and parcel of career advancement.

(2) Looking the other way is sometimes necessary to achieve success.

(3) Everyone does it, so if I don't do it as well then someone else will beat me to my goal.

(4) Business is business and its ethics are different from my personal ethics.

(5) It's not going to hurt anyone and it's not illegal, so why not do it?

(6) If others do not see through my deceptions then more fool them.

Most of the major situations that we have to face which involve ethical dilemmas will be created by, and thus correspond to, our dominant fears. The greater the fear, the more intense the situation will appear, with major ramifications for those involved; our keeping quiet, or not telling the truth, may affect someone's job, reputation, or feelings. We may be asked to lie in order to prevent a large sum of money being otherwise lost, and which in turn would mean we did not receive the promotion or contract that we had hoped for. It may be that we simply do not take the responsibility to resolve the harm that our mistakes have made.

It is usually our fears which govern the codes that are deemed part and parcel of success in business: we fear that if we respond differently from everyone else, we will not be liked, accepted, or asked to be involved. We fear that if we appear to be a threat to the status quo we will be passed over when it comes to promotion. We fear that we will fail if we follow a course of action that is compatible with our own sense of business ethics. We fear that confrontation, or encountering the disapproval of another, will threaten our job security, future contract or income.

Whatever our fears, until we confront them with our own sense of honesty, we will not release them and they will continue to plague us. We can be hurt by nothing; the hurt we feel stems from interpreting our dilemmas as proof that our fears are indeed valid. If we fail at something, or incur disapproval, this is outright proof that we are unworthy, incompetent, not good enough and unlovable. When we confront someone and incur their anger, this is proof that we must be wrong and they must be right. In truth, this is not proof that our fears are valid, only that we allow them to exist in our mind.

Confront and Conquer

Overcoming our fears means that any dilemmas that may arise in our lives disappear, as situations are perceived differently. Once again, however, what in truth is simple is often difficult to accept. The situations that each of us creates by our fears should be viewed as blessings, each with a role to play. All bring us the same opportunity to learn to release our fears and allow love to emerge in their place.

Each time you confront and conquer your fears you are allowing your true conscience to grow in influence. In doing so you avoid failures and, indeed, view any setbacks as valuable lessons when encountered. People with high self-esteem and no fears about their own worth are excellent people to work for and with.

As we release our fears, the confrontations that had

previously caused us pain become fewer, and the disapproval from others that made us feel so rejected becomes acceptable. This happens in direct proportion to our realisation that we cannot, and should not, try to please anyone by compromising our sense of worth and developing values. There is actually no such thing as a tense or uncomfortable situation with others. What has really bothered you is the behaviour and explanations you think you owe to others. You owe nothing to others except to be real, for you alone can give true value to yourself.

Trying to impress another, looking for approval, hanging on to someone's every word, expressing contrived concern for another's well-being, and explaining yourself, are all examples of you compromising your honesty with yourself. This is done in the false belief that you are strengthening your position with others. Being honest with yourself means never having to explain or complain.

By reminding yourself of the invalidity of your fears, as well as the benefits gained each time they are conquered, you will actually start to anticipate eagerly, rather than dread, those situations that allow you to confront them. Each time you confront and conquer your fear of being honest with yourself, you may still experience its reappearance. But its hold over you will be weaker and it will no longer be the dictator it was previously. It will simply be an emotion that you are aware of, but it can no longer influence you to discontinue the path that you know is right.

You will discover that you no longer use financial or career criteria as the dominant determinant in your decision-making. You will trust that if a deal does not happen or is lost, a better one will be lying on the path ahead of you. This path may appear painful at first, as it could appear to be a loss of something. But this sacrifice is an illusion, as any path that is grounded in integrity and balance will not only take you where you want to go, but provide peace of mind and fulfilment along the way. This path follows in union with the application of the third key.

Non-Justification of the 'I'

'Yao Kou, you promised last week that you would be here on time,' Tan Lee said to his partner. 'Yet you let me down again.'

'How so?' the astonished partner replied. 'Me, late? Well, I may not always be punctual, but I am never late! Anyway, it is not my fault. I had every intention of getting up earlier this morning but, upon waking, I noticed it was raining so I decided to wait awhile before leaving, as the market road would probably be awash. As it turned out it wasn't, so I am able to be here now as I said I would be, though I can't remember promising.'

'It is said that if you find it difficult to be sincere with yourself,' Tan Lee returned, 'it is not possible to be sincere with others.'

'Your trouble is that you always speak in riddles,' replied Yao Kou. 'What has sincerity got to do with it? It is simply that sometimes I find that the "I" that declares that he will rise early in the morning is different from the "I" that exists in the morning, who refuses to co-operate. Having so many different parts of him must be why a man, for instance, finds it so hard to keep something secret. First one "I" makes a promise, believing that he wants to keep the secret. Then tomorrow another "I" prompts him to tell his friend over a bottle of rice wine. With a different "I" in command, a clever person may question a man in such a way that he himself is unaware of what he is saying.'

'You're not trying to say that you have revealed what we discussed together last week are you?' enquired Tan Lee. 'We agreed that would remain between ourselves for the moment.'

'I met with the trader Fu'li, we drank and I couldn't help it. But I can't

say I'm sorry because it has been worth it. Fu'li raised doubts which I believe we should seriously consider. Anyway, it's hardly my fault. You should have made it clearer or at least given me all the facts.'

'I could not have made it clearer,' said Tan Lee. 'Yet listening to you reminds me of the teachings of that great sage who visited us from the West: "If one of thine 'I's offend thee, pluck it out." For without unity in your thinking you will continue to justify your own actions through blaming other people or things. It is clear that my "I" met with your wrong "I" last week, so all of me tells me I must depart. Goodbye.'

The New Testament reminds us that *If thine 'I' be single thy whole body shall be full of light.* In other words, only the true unified self is able to reveal its pure potential. A disunited self remains limited. This follows the holistic principle that the sum of the parts is greater than the Whole when brought together. When we are not in unity we will always seek to justify our actions. Yet by learning non-justification we are able to develop greater unity within ourselves. This in turn allows greater confidence.

The conditioned mind, formed by restrictive and limited thinking, does not want its false sense of security threatened by any unified thinking. So to prevent you from fully knowing yourself, it develops numerous 'I's and divides them into thought-proof walled compartments; we compartmentalise what is effectively the same emotional feeling about something. At one moment we feel one thing and at another something quite different. Each time you think '"I" will do this', this is later overridden by another 'I' occupying a different compartment that chooses to do something else. This 'I' in turn, has no dominion over the next 'I' resting in a further compartment.

Man, in his conditioned state, is a multiplicity of I's. Likening the unified self to a whole pound, then every moment you say 'I' you use a penny. Although we think we see the whole of something, we actually only allow ourselves to see a part because of the walled compartments we insist on putting everything into. Opinions and prejudices are examples of solid walls which we allow to become permanent through fixed ideas and misconceptions about ourselves. In turn, opinions and agendas, depending on the compartment, become chameleon-like, created to suit a particular situation or role. Unaware of their own agenda people can believe that 'they may not be always right, but they are never wrong.' Learning to become aware of our tendencies to label or pigeon-hole everything and everyone we meet, allows us to develop greater flexibility in our thinking, while trusting in our developing conscience.

Each of us experiences many different roles in life which make up our Whole 'I'. Each one of the 'I's delegates its duty to another, which in turn does not recognise the authority of the previous. Each separate 'I' is able to act, however, in the name of the Whole, to agree or disagree, to give promises and to make decisions with which another 'I' will have to deal. This explains why people so often make promises to themselves and so seldom carry them out.

The 'I' who decides to take time to consider what is really important in your life promises to start that very evening. The evening 'I' will take another view, however. This one will consider that the subject of your personal evaluation is far too important for you to do now, so chooses to defer the task until the weekend. In turn, the weekend 'I' to which the task has been delegated has other plans. After all, how can you spend a well deserved break doing something so important? This 'I' easily delegates to the future 'I' that will be in command on your holiday. It is no concern to the new 'I' what has been decided previously when it takes office, as former 'I' governments have no jurisdiction.

Raising Consciousness

An Eastern allegory compares Man to a house full of servants whose master and head steward are absent. As the servants forget their roles and do what they like, with no co-ordination, the house ends up in complete chaos. The only possibility for things to improve is for a number of servants to agree to appoint a deputy steward. The elected steward can then command the other servants to do the right work in the right place. There is then every possibility of the head steward returning to replace the deputy and to prepare the house for the master's return. The master can be likened to your true self, which can only appear when the level of consciousness of knowing who you are has been attained. As the unified true self once more takes command from your disunited conditioned self, you no longer feel the need to compartmentalise everything to fit previous preconceptions.

This is a level of consciousness that does not seek justification for any of your actions. Being in a unified state of mind allows you to follow the counsel of your own heart and live the life you're intended to live by making your own decisions, rather than passively submitting to what others think is best for you. This will involve putting yourself first, which of course runs contrary to what we have been taught.

The truth is that to be sincere with others we must first develop sincerity in ourselves. There can be no other choice, in the area of personal development, than to put ourselves first. This does not mean running roughshod over others; it involves consciously accepting that only you have the power to make yourself either happy or unhappy. In making yourself happy you are able to create happiness for others because your increased self-esteem does not need to justify itself. Only when you have made sense of yourself can you then make sense of the surrounding world.

Becoming conscious of our habitual tendency to be judgmental towards others, or to seek justification for our own actions, allows us to tune into our true conscience. This allows us to have a bird's eye view of all our different compartments and reveals to us how we really feel about something.

Becoming conscious of those times when we feel we have to justify ourselves provides us with the opportunity to dissolve a false 'I' and instead listen to the guiding voice of a surer, developed conscience.

The Winning Corner

At one time or another, everyone feels that they have been a rat. Whenever we have behaved badly, particularly in relationships, we put it down, in all honesty, to our acting out of character. 'I can't believe I said that!' we exclaim, or 'Was that person really me?', or 'I just wasn't myself.' Our conscience therefore seems to work best whenever we are being observed by another. How much better it would be if we could begin to observe ourselves as another might.

Harnessing our true conscience through: fully understanding our motives, before making a move; being honest with ourselves as to what is really important to us so that we are not prepared to compromise, regardless of persuasion; not feeling that we have to justify our actions, because we have the confidence that they have been initiated by a more unified self, provides the power that will unerringly guide us towards balanced growth and development. Our ultimate goal is for peace of mind. Everything that is meant for us and our highest good, be it a job, promotion, a relationship, or a sum of money, and every action that leads us to what is right for us, will come from listening to our true conscience. Whatever *dis*comfort we experience will derive from behaviour based on false fears.

Whenever circumstances demand a compromise from you, take the opportunity to re-examine your motives to resolve any fears you may have. If you feel you are having to compromise your true conscience, accept it as an indication that you need to alter your circumstances, perhaps leave a relationship. Beware of looking for the angle in everything, as in doing so you place yourself in uncomfortably tight corners, and drain yourself of energy in fighting to get out. But remember that while one of the most painful wounds in the world is a stab of conscience, it is good that you always win, because it may otherwise disfigure the soul.

The Sixth Scroll: Seeing the Snake

The Secret of Reaching Heightened Awareness and Open Concentration

Several people were walking along the north road to Han Tan early one morning when they each came upon a man lying in the roadside. The first person, pausing in his journey, said out loud, 'That man must be drunk and sleeping it off, probably after gambling all night at the Mah Jong House I'll wager. The scoundrel ought to know when he's had enough and go home, rather than sleeping where it suits him!' Continuing on his way he shouted, 'The gutter is the best place for you.'

A second passer-by said worriedly to himself, 'He could be dead, having been bitten by a poisonous snake. There are some venomous ones in these parts I hear.' Hurrying ahead he soon overtook the first man.

'Poor unfortunate,' thought a third person, a little later. 'He must be very ill and looks as though he doesn't want to be disturbed. I'd better let him rest where he is.'

A fourth man following soon after, thought, 'That must be a travelling holy man, one who is above ordinary physical consciousness. What austere clothes he wears and a strange stick he has. And that net sacking that surrounds him appears most uncomfortable. But then such a saintly man can meditate anywhere, be it a ditch or a temple, sitting or lying. I must be careful not to disturb him.' And bowing, he too carried on.

Meanwhile, the first man had caught up with the second, who had previously passed him. The first had not spoken to the second earlier because he had felt the man was not worth talking to. 'What's that scoundrel hiding, hurrying like that?' he remembered thinking. The second man was motioning for silence with one hand to his lips while pointing with the other to something half on the road and half hidden in the undergrowth.

'Look there,' he whispered. 'It's a snake, just as I thought. And by the look of its orange and black markings it is lethal.'

'It looks more like a bit of coloured binding rope to me,' the first man said. 'There are many merchants passing here and that's been dumped there by some scoundrel I expect.'

'Still, to be on the safe side,' said the second, 'let us together throw a heavy rock and trap whatever it is.'

It was half an hour before the other walkers discovered to their horror the remains of two badly mauled bodies lying in the road. Both had seemingly died in a bloody instant. While desperately wondering what dreadful fate had befallen the unfortunates, they were soon joined by the man they had earlier seen lying in the roadside.

'Am I too late?' the newcomer shouted breathlessly. 'Did any of you see which way the beast went?'

'Beast, what beast?' shouted the others in terror. 'Quickly tell us what devil is living in these parts?'

'It is no devil,' replied the man. 'It is the mascot of Chao. I am Third Keeper Mo Kop, protector of General Li Mu's leopard. The Cat Beast is a treasured gift that escaped two days ago and I, among others, have pursued it without rest. Until last night that is, when, desperate for rest from my exhaustion, I must have collapsed at the side of this road. Now I'm ravenous. Have you any food?'

'Food! How can you think of food! What about these unfortunates? And what are you doing letting such a beast out in civilised parts? This is Sung Province, not Chao. What right has one of your Generals got to bring death here?'

'The same right that you have to travel to Han Tan, capital of Chao,'

answered Mo Kop, flatly. 'And as for these poor devils, well, they must have chanced upon the leopard while it too was asleep, though for it to set upon them is strange. It must have thought they were attacking it, for it has never reacted before in this way. Oh dear, I can see already that if the mascot is in any way hurt I will be made to pay dearly! Oh woe am I, and it was not even my fault the beast escaped. Still,' added Mo Kop, brightening up as he ran off, 'by my ancestors, at least it is not First and Second Keeper lying here, as I first thought. Perhaps with good fortune they are at this moment recapturing our mascot!'

The world, as each of us perceives it, is nothing but our own projection. We see what we expect to see because the way we perceive is based on our individual frame of reference, formed by our conditioning, through which we interpret everything we experience. And what we perceive has to fit, for if not, we just don't see it. People will always see what they have decided to see, construing their world according to how it should be, rather than how it is.

The scoundrel, therefore, sees a scoundrel; the drinker sees a drunk; the worrier sees problems; the saint bows to a saint. Yet all are mistaken. Where one sees what his frame of reference perceives to be a snake, another sees something dumped by a scoundrel, yet both are unaware that it is really the tail of a dangerous animal. If heaven and hell are states of consciousness that we allow ourselves to occupy, then if there is hell in your mind, you won't see heaven anywhere. If there is heaven in your mind, you can't see hell.

Because of our fixed frames of reference, our tendency is to *prejudge*, or have prejudice against, anything that does not fit our expectations. Our perceptions distort our beliefs, our values, our commitments and our communications with others. Unaware that they may be inaccurate we react with cynicism or are sceptical when confronted with anything that lies outside our frame of reference. Too often the refrain of: 'If only I had been aware of that', has escaped the lips of either the hasty person, who causes unnecessary stress or anguish through jumping to conclusions; or the immovable person, who overlooks opportunity through their refusing to be flexible. It doesn't have to be this way and, as all missed opportunities and misunderstandings spring from our inaccurate perceptions, it shouldn't be this way.

Waking up to the fact that we are blinkered is the first positive step in gaining awareness. It often takes a shock of some kind, however, for this to happen. Whatever the shock, be it personal or professional, there is always a positive side effect should we choose to use it to gain greater awareness. In reaching a higher level of awareness we gain significant rewards and are able to achieve much more while expending less energy. Too often we tend to continue to get the same results, because we continue to do those things that we have always unconsciously done. In other words, if we carry on doing what we've always done, we'll carry on getting what we've always got. The alternative, being consciously aware of whatever we do, brings greater achievement for less effort; it is not the hours you put in that count, it is what you put into the hours. Or, put another way, one insight will resolve a thousand difficulties.

Being aware gives you the ability to develop open concentration. Lack of concentration is the cause of most accidents, so the ability to concentrate is fundamental to survival. But open concentration is far and above ordinary concentration. It is the ability to bring focused attention to what you are involved with, while remaining conscious of what is happening around you.

Many people believe that meditation, a growing practice in the West, is a form of concentration. Any meditation, however, that leads you deep into concentration makes you more and more closed rather than open. Whenever you narrow down your consciousness you become unmindful of the surrounding world. Where the scientist, for instance, becomes absent-minded because he is concentrating on the problem in hand, the great sage is not a man of closed concentration, he is a man of awareness. In being so unaware, the scientist may hit on the point but miss the greater picture. Concentration makes you single-focused at great cost — all other aspects of life are ignored. Open concentration takes everything in and is thus infinitely more effective.

Concentration involves focusing the mind on form; contemplation involves focusing the mind on an idea; meditation involves raising consciousness. Working in harmony the three are able to create a state of relaxed intensity which allows clear perception, creativity and focused attention to come together. This heightened awareness will naturally allow you to focus on what you know is clearly the right direction, while creatively harnessing all the opportunities and situations that you accurately perceive around you. Application and practice of certain keys are fundamental to reaching this state.

Observing Self-Evaluation

'I would be honoured to assist your Greatness in this matter,' said Chih-Po, rushing forward.

Counsellor Tang turned in the direction of his approaching assistant and asked, 'Are you aware of the difficulties associated with such a business as this?'

'Listening to you, your Worship, has provided me with the knowledge associated with such a business as this,' answered the bowing courtier. 'You just have to instruct me on the outcome that you want and I will see that it will be done.'

'Even if what I might want may cause rifts for the people or business concerned?' questioned Tang.

'Although a humble assistant counsellor, my Lord, I am a teacher, and as such believe myself to be a good judge of character. I do not have to meet the men to whom you refer, to be of the opinion that, as they have brought such consternation to one so revered, their actions must be in question. As such, any injury that I or another may give to them is simply their due brought on by themselves.'

'Well, I know these men involved and I believe them to be good, which is why I am questioning my own thinking,' Counsellor Tang commented.

'Of course, your Honour,' replied Chih-Po. 'Allow me to visit them in going about their business so that I can report to you ...'

'Enough!' interrupted Counsellor Tang. 'How can you evaluate others when you yourself possess the eight faults and apply the four evils that beset the undertakings of all men?' And turning to the advisor on his right he said, 'Chang, remind this "judge of character" that anyone knowing themselves must examine each one carefully.'

'Yes Counsellor,' replied Chang who, turning to face Chih-Po, proceeded to do so. 'To do what is not your business to do is called officiousness. To rush forward when your comments are unsolicited is obsequiousness. To echo a man's opinions and try to draw him out in speech is called sycophancy. To speak without regard for what is right or wrong is called flattery. To delight in talking about other men's failings is called calumny. To break up friendships and set kinsfolk at odds is called maliciousness. To praise falsely and hypocritically so as to cause injury and evil to others is called wickedness. Without thought for right or wrong, to try and steal a glimpse of the other party's wishes is called treachery. These eight faults inflict chaos on others and injury on the possessor.

'As for the four evils,' continued Chang, 'to be fond of plunging into great undertakings to enhance your merit and fame is called avidity. To insist that you know it all, that everything be done your way, snatching from others and appropriating for your own use, this is called avarice. To see your errors but refuse to change, to listen to remonstrance but go on behaving worse than *before, this is called obstinacy. When men agree with you, to commend them; when they disagree with you, to see no goodness in them when it is there, this is called bigotry.'*

'So,' spoke Counsellor Tang. 'When you, Teacher Chih-Po, can do away with the eight faults and avoid committing the four evils, then and only then will you become capable of being taught. Before any man is qualified to evaluate another he must first be capable of being taught self-evaluation. Until that time you are dismissed, for I have no need of services such as yours!'

Although never a day passes without our evaluating others, very few of us ever evaluate ourselves. Common sense tells us that we cannot evaluate another before we are able to evaluate ourselves, yet common practice proves otherwise. Judging the character of another is not a question of social status or seniority, though many people believe their 'position' enables them to evaluate someone quickly. However, these same people have never evaluated themselves using the same criteria with which they evaluate others.

Those people who are responsible for regularly evaluating or appraising others will readily admit, if asked, that to be qualified to evaluate another you first need to have evaluated your own thoughts and actions. Yet how many of them will want to admit that they have never actually done so themselves? Think for a moment about the people in the area in which you live and the people you meet and work with: neighbours, colleagues, friends, customers, guests, new acquaintances and relatives. Consider the time you spend evaluating, appraising, analysing, assessing, considering or judging them. Now take a moment to reflect on the following: how much of each day do you spend in self-evaluation?

Daily self-evaluation is the vital key to awakening your self-awareness. It is no use trying to imagine what awakened self-awareness is like before it is attained. Approach it the other way and see the result that non-awareness has on your life. Being unaware is like thinking that tomorrow will be different while you inwardly remain the same. Outer change demands inner change, and only through self-evaluation can we begin to see how to do things in a new way, a way that is beneficial. Nothing beneficial, however, can ever happen to us until we see something about ourselves that we were previously unaware of. Rather than ask, 'what can I do so that I can at last be happy?', we can ask, 'what can I give up doing so that I can cease being unhappy?'

Self-evaluation does not mean asking the opinions of others because there is always 'me as I am', and 'me as I want others to think I am'. But regardless of the fact that our true aware self is the best friend and advisor we will ever have, we still tend to ask others — 'what do *you* think I should do?' rather than 'what must *I* do?' The questions we ask ourselves should be those that come so freely to us when silently evaluating others. For example, the next time you feel upset because you are not in control of a situation, ask yourself why you really need to have control. When someone annoys you because they always want the last word, ask yourself why it is that you are annoyed. Is it that you need to have the last word?

Becoming aware involves standing outside of ourselves and observing everything that happens to us, both inside and out. In the same way that you have probably noticed how others fidget, drum their fingers or tap their feet, start to observe your own physical actions. Notice how you were unaware of them before.

Many people unwittingly caught on camera are surprised to see how they fidget or gesture in a certain way, being previously unaware of it. When confronted with our behaviour, we are often surprised at the way we project ourselves to others. It is not some special gift for others to see us differently to the way we see ourselves, it is simply that we do not make the effort, or take the time, to be as aware of ourselves as we are of others.

Reacting and Responding

In the same way that we are aware of drinking hot or cold water, we can begin to observe our internal conditions by learning to distinguish between situations that cause us to become comfortably cool or disturbingly hot. Observing how we react or respond to people and circumstances teaches us to address, rather than repress, the very cause of our reaction or response. Just the action of doing this leads us to greater self-awareness. The difference between reacting and responding is that in the former state you are not in control, whereas in the latter you are. It is important to register this difference because at any one moment in your life you are either in command of yourself or not. There is no neutral.

Take the rejection or acceptance by another of what we do, for example. When another accepts us we respond positively. We feel in command because we feel needed, worthy and valued. If, however, we are rejected and react negatively, it is because we feel unwanted, unworthy and unvalued. Unless we are aware that we are *re*acting to rejection we will merely repress whatever causes the feeling, thus inviting it to affect us whenever a similar situation threatens us. The very fact that we can be aware of our reaction, however, gives us the means to address it, thus destroying what causes it for ever. This follows the principle that to remove an illness you must first diagnose it. Awareness teaches us that we can actually learn more from rejection than from acceptance, in the same way that a missile stays on target because its gyro rejects a wrong direction.

Being Casually Alert

The real art of effective contemplation is two-fold. It involves observing how the actions or emotions of others affect and influence you, and how your own actions and emotions affect others. Through consistent daily practice of observing how others react or respond, you can correct the actual causes which stem from your current thinking. Contemplation itself is the culmination of self-evaluation and detached observation.

Imagine you have dug a perfect hole. Now imagine you are simply passing a hole that someone else has dug, and as you do so you pause to inspect the hole. You are more dispassionate about the second hole because you have not dug it. The key is to try and imagine the first action with the emotion of the second. Any hole we dig ourselves into will always come from our own thinking, so being able to dispassionately contemplate why we have dug a hole and why we continue to put ourselves in it, enables us not only to get out of it but to fill it in for good.

All negative thinking about ourselves will disappear unless it is held on to and given non-existent value. Dispassionate contemplation allows you to discard harmful thoughts from your mind in the same way that you discard out-of-date food. The increasing freedom you gain from ridding yourself of self-defeating thoughts allows you to think more clearly. Clarity of thinking is fundamental to becoming aware of your inner world, and the more you understand your inner world the less your outer world can hurt you. Building greater awareness in your life requires you to be watchful of your daily affairs. This means learning to be *casually alert* in all things which, in turn, requires contemplation brought together with the elements of the second key.

Focused Attention

After twenty years in the service of a provincial overlord, a loyal soldier was rewarded. With enough money now to buy some acres of land, he was excited at being able to realise his dream of building his own home. For three whole months the soldier totally absorbed himself in preparing the land, clearing it of boulders and levelling the ground. He made sure that any wild bushes and neglected growth removed were replaced with trees and flowers. The work was long and hard, but the soldier felt richly rewarded by thinking how pleasant his home would be.

While engrossed in what he was doing, a man came up to him and introduced himself as the land agent in the service of the local registrar.

'What so,' said the soldier, taking the opportunity to rest. 'How can I be of service to you? All is well I trust?'

'I'm not sure,' said the man, looking puzzled. 'Might I please enquire as to who has employed you on such obvious land improvement?'

'I am now in the service of my own,' replied the soldier proudly. 'I am the owner of this land. I am preparing it for building.'

'There seems to have been some mistake,' said the land agent, holding out a sheaf of papers with some consternation. 'This is not your land, I'm afraid. Your land comprises the acres actually adjoining this.'

'Ah,' sighed the soldier. 'So, despite my endeavours I have not done a single thing to improve my own property.' And with that he immediately set to gathering his tools. The soldier took the mistake in good spirit, and after making sure that he was on his own land, he once more earnestly set about making his dream come true.

If we are unaware that we are running down the wrong road then our attention to how fast we are running is irrelevant. Most times, though, we will not admit to ourselves that we are on the wrong road, so our thinking is never reversed and we continue to plough over old ground. Having attention in itself is a good discipline as it builds our ability to concentrate. But a difficult fact to accept is that one moment of awareness in the right ground, is a thousand times better than one year of concentrated effort in the wrong ground. The 'wrong ground' denotes any attraction which distracts us from self-awareness.

The soldier in the story was so attracted to working towards his dream that he was distracted from ensuring that he was working the right land. When his error was pointed out, however, he immediately went to work without seeking redress for his error. And here is a vital truth, for when you are able to hear that all your work has been in vain without being angry, then you are on the path to self-awareness. Being able to focus your attention on what you should be doing, immediately you are aware of it, is preferable to the more common reaction of focusing attention on who was to blame for you not being aware.

When people feel humiliation for having been cheated by others, for example, what really humiliates them is having their gullibility exposed. But a willingness to learn by being aware of why they feel the pain will remove their gullibility. Most people do the opposite, however, blaming external situations for their pain and seeking recompense to remove their humiliation. In doing so they merely trade the pain of the humiliation for the pain of resentment and anger.

Blaming external conditions and other people for the way we feel is a major distraction from focusing on what we really want to do. Concentrating obsessively on making another pay for what we think they have done to us is the exact opposite of open concentration. It narrows our attention, drawing to us only those negative elements that will allow us to get our own back or make someone pay.

When it comes to concentrating, our minds seem to follow the movements of a snake — in order to travel straight ahead it moves from side to side. The span of our concentration on something that does not hold our attention is very short. This is usually because we are not aware of what it is that holds our attention. For example, a child's school report may declare that the child is unable to concentrate in class for two minutes without difficulty. This is the same child, however, that can concentrate endlessly on playing a game they have invented for themselves. It is simply that the latter holds their attention.

Becoming aware as to when it is an effort to concentrate on something does not mean you should try harder to concentrate, it means acknowledging that what you are doing does not hold your attention. This is a clear opportunity to take the time to discover why. It may be that you are plain lazy. If that is the case then acknowledging it, rather than denying it, is the thing to do, as opportunities that are right for us begin to show up because our honest consciousness is ready for them, and as we are aware we notice them. A lazy person is often more innovative because they look to achieve things with the least possible effort.

Alternatively, your attention may be reduced simply because you have either lost interest, or were never interested in the first place. Often we refuse to be aware of this as it means acknowledging that we do what we do solely because of our commitments.

Working at something because we *have* to, rather than because we *want* to, is definitely working the wrong ground. Putting good money into something that has failed in order to make it work is often viewed as something we have to do. With our attention on getting back what we may have lost, we concentrate on keeping whatever it is afloat. Being aware that it is not really what we want, however, can allow us to give it up by recognising that our efforts are not serving any other purpose than maintaining our obstinacy or pride. Do not confuse these characteristics with persistence and determination as these qualities are vital for achievement. The point is that unless we are fully aware of the emotions driving us, we may end up at the wrong destination.

A state of heightened awareness allows us to ensure that we do not compromise what is best for us by accepting only what is good. Having a 'good' job yet disliking it, is clearly not the 'best'. Concentrating on what is best for you has infinitely more focus than concentrating on what is just good. For example, concentrating your efforts on ensuring you can provide everything for your family may be at the expense of spending time together as a family; concentrating your efforts to ensure that you receive a promotion or contract may not be in your best health interests. What is perceived as best will, of course, be up to the individual's level of awareness.

When something does hold your attention and absorbs you, then all ripple effects will be in your best interests because, in fully expressing yourself, you are 'walking your talk'. In this way your self-awareness, independent will, creative imagination and conscience are all acting in harmony.

Thinking Seriously Lightly

As the best way of observing yourself is to be casually alert, then the best way to develop open concentration while focusing your attention is to take things *seriously lightly*. A state of heightened awareness does not recognise these as opposite concepts; they are the most natural and productive way of addressing everything. To think seriously lightly means to think from a position of understanding, rather than from the memories of past experiences. A person might think seriously about losing a job, for example, but by resenting redundancy they rob themselves of thinking lightly, which could have produced peaceful understanding. Each time you consent to a loss, rather than resent it, expect a gain.

The next time you have to concentrate on something important, first become aware of how you will feel about it. Take time to contemplate what you are about to do in order to establish if it is important to you as well as interesting and absorbing. If your thoughts are positive then commence work in the full expectation that you will gain immense benefit from it.

If your thoughts are negative, then contemplate why. It may be that you hunger for the credit rather than the personal satisfaction of seeing the venture through. If this is the case, by becoming aware of your need for recognition, you remove the distraction of it. You may become aware that this is not the way to proceed at all, in which case you have saved yourself further wasted effort. The numerous permutations of the truth will become clear to you, as long as you are self-aware.

In actually applying your powers of concentration, go seriously lightly. In this way you will appreciate the whole of what you are doing and will not close yourself off from the surrounding elements that are part and parcel of the task in hand. Too serious and you will not see the wood for the trees. Too light and you will see the wood without knowing the species of tree. For example, the proofreader who is concentrating purely on grammatical errors does not know the content of the book; the closeted judge concentrating on the psychology of the criminal mind has no time to understand human nature; the religious scholar concentrating on performing rites and rituals overlooks spirituality; the businessman concentrating on satisfying his shareholders never has time to meet his customers. Approaching everything with a seriously light attitude leads us to the application of the third key.

Witnessing Your Thoughts and Actions

A woman travelled to the great lake at Shura Province to seek the advice of a renowned sage. Granting her an audience, he enquired what she sought from him.

'*I am here because my husband has talked of you with great respect,*' *began the woman.* '*So, if I return with advice from yourself he may perhaps listen to it.*'

'*A man will only listen when he is ready to listen,*' *commented the sage,* '*but you have travelled far, so tell me the problem you have.*'

'*My husband is a high court judge. But he remains so every moment, even in bed. I have not known a lover, friend or husband. He is always so proud of how aware and alert he is of everything and everyone, yet for twenty-four hours a day he is aware of nothing, except being a high court judge. It is said that you have the power to allow people to see themselves as others do. Please can you help me?*'

'*Often the height of the pedestal prevents removal from it,*' *began the sage,* '*whatever a person does, be they a scholar, merchant or Emperor. But I will help you. Return and tell him that you have received word, albeit from my own lips, that I have heard of his respect for me and will therefore pay my own to him soon.*'

Hearing the news that such a renowned sage would be visiting his house, the high court judge placed a sentry to give him early warning of his arrival. '*It is because he has heard of my alert mind that he is visiting,*' *he told his colleagues, while inviting them to come also.*

The town merchants and scholars looked forward to the day. The clerks to the judge felt more important than before as they answered the townspeople's questions: '*Of course such a sage will not visit just anyone, you know. The reputation of our master's wisdom goes far and wide, for there are none that challenge it.*'

When the sentry reported that a stranger asking where the high court judge lived had entered the town, word quickly spread and within the hour the House of Justice was bursting at the seams.

But the stranger was not the sage. He was a simpleton who, when questioned, replied that he had been sent ahead by the sage to test the judge's renowned wisdom. If the judge answered four questions from the simpleton incorrectly then the sage would come. If, however, the judge, was to answer any of the questions correctly, then the judge would lose the test and the sage would not come.

'Some test,' thought the judge. 'Answering incorrectly is far easier than answering correctly. How can I lose with this confused simpleton?' Then, speaking out loud for the benefit of all, he said, 'Begin your test, ask your questions, all of which I will answer incorrectly for you. When I pass you must bring your master and should I lose, well, if I were to, I would even give you ten gold coins from my own purse.'

So the simpleton began, and asked, 'Where do you come from?'

The judge said, 'From Chao Province,' which was incorrect as he had always lived in Shura Province. 'There,' he said, 'I have passed the first test,' winking at his clerks.

'How long have you been here?' asked the simpleton for his second question.

'Two weeks only,' replied the judge, who had lived there all his life, among growing laughter as people began to join in the joke.

The third time the simpleton asked, 'Our courts are fair and just in this province. Do you agree?'

'Not at all,' answered the judge. 'Our courts are the worst in all China,' again passing the test.

'It seems that you can't lose,' said the simpleton. 'You are as aware as they say you are. How many questions have I asked so far?'

The judge said, 'You have asked me three questions; you have one more. If I do not answer it correctly I pass your master's tests.'

'Look!' cried out the simpleton, jumping up and down with excitement. 'The judge has failed the test. He has answered this question correctly! You

see, even when great judges are not alert they lose. Had he been more aware
he would have passed the test.'

Having his pride smashed in front of his peer group had an enormous
impact on the judge. In the silence that engulfed the entire room, he momentarily
entered a trance-like state where he became a witness to the whole event. He
did not feel a victim, he was simply witnessing the absurdity of what had
been a false self. One that relied on a pedestal, title, respect and importance.
Returning to his quarters later, the high court judge felt as if a huge burden
had been lifted from him. He became aware of the warm welcome from his
wife as he opened the door.

This story illustrates one of the most important secrets of
fulfilment – the ability to witness ourselves, rather than judge.
Everybody is capable of reaping the infinite benefits available, yet
most don't even get close to it; we are too busy judging others.
Although each of us carries the key to the door of fulfilment,
very few ever turn the lock. All that is required, however, is to
take the time to meditate.

Sitting cross-legged and half-naked under a tree humming
to yourself is not meditation. Millions of people miss out on
meditation because of its false connotation. They think it is
gloomy and serious, or religious and monastic, or downright
weird and bizarre. Yet meditation affords the opportunity to
embark on the greatest adventure the human mind can take. In
truth, total awareness is a form of meditation.

To meditate means to become a witness. That is the whole
secret of meditation – you become the watcher of whatever you
are doing. Action is not the purpose, but the quality that you
bring to your action. Walking, sitting, running, jogging and
swimming are all forms of meditation if you remain alert.
Meditation is a quality that can be brought to anything, it
is not a specific act. The common belief, however, is that
it must be a specific act; you must sit facing east, repeat

certain mantras, burn some incense in a particular way at a particular time. Meditation has nothing to do with anything that seeks to automate it because it is not about automation, it is about alertness. So long as you are alert, any activity can be a meditation.

The key to meditating does involve a *knack*. A knack is not a science or an art; it cannot be taught. But effort is required to acquire the knack. Learning to swim or ride a bike takes initial effort before it becomes natural. When you have the knack, however, you never forget, despite any infrequency of use. Regular swimming or cycling will obviously improve ability but once you have 'clicked' with how to maintain buoyancy or balance respectively, what was once a locked door is always open to you. All of us, in fact, are natural swimmers from birth, but false fears make us unaware of this. We are afraid of drowning so we seek a technique in order to *learn* how to swim. Babies and small children who are completely unafraid of the water swim in moments, others with just an ounce of concern do not.

Although meditation is not in itself a technique, there are numerous techniques to achieve the heightened awareness that it brings. You could learn by yourself, but the journey may be tedious and boring. Techniques used in thousands of years of experiments can certainly save you unnecessary groping about and propel your growth immensely. If after trying one for a few days, nothing 'clicks', then try another. You will know when one is right for you as you will feel right about using it.

Effort will still be required, though, so you should continue with it. But only in the beginning will meditating seem like an effort. When you succeed, the effort disappears and the event becomes spontaneous, like breathing. Effort is always required in the beginning because the mind will not start anything without it. A moment will come, however, when through your effort, you completely relax and effortlessly become a witness. In this meditative state, you are beyond the thinker in you, beyond what you are doing, you are just aware.

Looking at the whole of something is an example of awareness. Whenever we look at an object or person, unconsciously we only look at the parts. Taking a bowl of fruit, for example. We move our eyes to look at the sides, then to what it contains, then to the substance. By refusing to allow our eyes to divide what they see into parts, however, we force them to see something as a whole. Try it. First look at any object, a wall picture perhaps. Notice how you look from one part to another. Then suddenly look at it as a whole; do not divide it. Do not allow your eyes to move. Do not think; forget the substance, material or what the frame is made of, just look at the form.

Go on looking at the form as a whole, and in a few moments you become aware of yourself. You become aware of yourself while looking at something else because your eyes are not allowed to move outwards. The form has been taken as a whole, so you cannot move to the parts. As the eyes demand movement, so your vision will move towards you. It will come back and suddenly you will become aware of watching yourself watch the object. This will give you an indication of what being a witness rather than a judge involves. This awareness of your self is incomparable to any other experience.

Starting to Meditate

It is important when you are new to meditation to allow yourself enough time and to find a peaceful place. The half-hour you take out of your twenty-four-hour day will prove to be more valuable to you than the rest, although you may not believe it now. Certainly tranquillity is important so you may prefer to rise earlier than usual in order to enjoy some quiet time alone. A whole group of people can meditate together when they have genuine motives to gain higher awareness, otherwise distractions will occur. When a person has really learned to meditate, however, they can meditate anywhere and anytime with no concern of distraction.

When meditating without moving, your posture should be such that you forget your body, because then you know you are comfortable. To maintain alertness it is better to sit upright, as if you lie down you will fall asleep. Many people take up a cross-legged yoga position which is fine if it is comfortable. In the East all children grow up sitting like this on a daily basis and so it is a most comfortable position for them. In the West, however, we do not, so the rule is to sit however you like as long as you are comfortable, while keeping your back straight and your head firmly balanced. All ancient methods of meditation were developed in the East without consideration of the Western population, but the two distinct types listed below have proved to be highly successful for people from all walks of life.

Vipassana

Vipassana is a form of meditation that has led more people to a state of heightened awareness than any other. It is pure essence, so not being able to add or subtract anything from it means you can only improve it. It is so simple that even a small child can do it. In fact he or she, not yet exposed to life's prejudices, can do it better.

As nothing during the meditation is considered a distraction, it is ideal for many beginners. There are a number of ways in which it can be done; choose whichever of the two following methods suits you best. The first involves awareness of your breathing, while the second involves awareness of your body, your mind and your mood.

Breathing

Adopt a comfortable and alert position in which to sit for thirty minutes. Your back and head should be straight, eyes closed, and breathing normal. This means breathing down to the stomach, not through raising the chest. If you are uncertain, practise lying on the floor with your hand just above your navel. When it rises up and down you are breathing correctly. Your focus of attention should be on watching the rise and fall of your stomach caused by the in and out of your breathing.

If you are distracted by anything, including thoughts, feelings, judgements, body sensations and impressions from the outside world, pay attention to whatever is happening until it is possible to focus your breathing again. It is the process of watching that is important, not what you are watching, so do not identify with whatever your thoughts are. Problems and questions should pass like ships on the horizon. It is only when you identify with a ship that you feel distressed. If you say 'that is my ship', you will worry as soon as it passes from sight. When negative ideas arise just watch them and let them go.

Body, Mind and Mood

This involves a slow, ordinary walk, focusing on your feet touching the ground. You can walk in a circle or a line of ten to fifteen steps back and forth, inside or out of doors. Your eyes should be focused on the ground a few steps ahead. While walking, your focus of attention should be on the contact of each foot as it touches the ground. If you are diverted, stop paying attention to the feet, notice what else took your attention and then return to the feet. Walk for twenty to thirty minutes.

Zazen

Zen meditators don't do anything, they just sit. Doing absolutely nothing is hard, but once you have the knack many things will begin to happen. At first, and possibly for several weeks or months, incessant thoughts of the pointlessness of what you are doing, will enter your mind. 'How can you waste so much time, when you could be earning money?' your mind will demand. 'You could at least do something, even if it is just watching TV. Entertain yourself, this is absurd.'

Your mind will do all that it can to stop you from just sitting. It will make you sleepy, or want to move, or come up with a million arguments and reasons for not staying put. But if you can just persevere, the mind eventually stops its haranguing and a sense of silence and peace enters you which is total. You have entered God, you have entered truth.

You can sit anywhere as long as you are not distracted – in front of a plain wall is ideal. Adopt a good posture, ensuring that you settle and are able to stay as still as possible for thirty minutes. This is important because if the body does not move, the mind automatically falls silent as they are one energy. Your eyes should be half open, allowing your gaze to rest softly on the wall, and your breathing should be relaxed. Rest one hand inside the other with the thumbs touching and ensure that your back is straight. Place your attention at a spot behind the centre of your forehead, where the pineal gland is located, but do not concentrate. Remain relaxed while becoming as receptive and alert as possible from moment to moment.

Enlightening yourself

Understandably, meditation will seem difficult at first but the results are worth the effort. Although everyone is capable of enjoying its rewards, few choose to persevere with it. The key to doing so is patience and not looking for immediate results. The very nature of meditation is non-goal-orientated, so more than anything else, the meditator has to work on the process without attachment to the result. At times impatience will come, as impatience always comes with the thirst for achievement. But the meditator must learn to throw away impatience while keeping his or her thirst. With thirst there is yearning but no struggle; with impatience there is struggle but no yearning. Truth cannot be raided; it is attained through surrender, not through struggle.

Absolutely nothing masters the unruly mind more effectively than meditation. Command of your mind, and being aware of your thinking, will determine your success in everything you undertake. But how can the aeons of heritage, tradition, conditioning and prejudice that have allowed the mind to believe it is the master of you rather than your servant, be overcome just by doing nothing and watching? It can, because like the night watchman keeping thieves at bay with his light, destructive thoughts are vanquished when they are seen for what they are. A negative thought is like a thief, it does not like to be in the spotlight. As the watcher grows stronger and more aware he becomes at one with the strengthening light his awareness brings. That is the meaning of enlightenment. At one with the Light. At one with the Truth.

Relaxed Intensity

Observing yourself through self-evaluation, focusing your attention through open concentration and witnessing your thoughts and actions through meditation are the valuable keys to creating a state of *relaxed intensity*. Here again, higher consciousness does not recognise opposites, it sees them as complementary energies. Concentration itself is the key to all aspects of life. The more you concentrate on what you do, the more you begin to live in the present. Whenever you lack concentration you are easily distracted from living in the present, and distractions are the enemy of awareness.

When you increase your levels of concentration you begin to see yourself in a more valuable light. You are able to rechannel your nervous energy, using it to work with you, not against you. But the true power of concentration is the ability to become a witness to your own being. To achieve this the mind must be in a state of calmness. This means that you have to be able to relax while at the same time intensifying your energy in order that it becomes focused. Meditation is calmness, not doing; concentration is intensity, doing. One is not the other but together they create a state of relaxed intensity.

Action through non-action and doing without doing is ancient wisdom. Each complements the other, making the whole stronger. Remember that concentration is the focusing of the mind on form; contemplation is the focusing of the mind on an idea; and meditation is raising of the consciousness. Spending time on each regularly will allow you to reach a level of awareness that will prove enlightening to you in all aspects of perception, situations, opportunities and witnessing.

As you shine the light of attention back in on yourself, rather than on external devices and skills which are only visible reflections of yourself, your whole sense of perspective will be clearer. You will know the direction to take in all matters, opportunities will come to you without effort, and you will know what to do with them.

The Seventh Scroll: Shooting the Monkey

The Secret of Gaining Freedom from the Distracting Ego

猴

Invited to a grand reception, Chang did not dress for the occasion. Arriving in his everyday clothes he was treated with disrespect and contempt. No-one paid him any attention and the servants did their utmost to ignore him, not even serving him dinner. Slipping out unnoticed, Chang went home and changed into the finest silk tunic, belt and robes adorned with breath-taking jewellery, a magnificent turban and an expensive overcoat. Returning to the banquet he was received with open arms. Although all harboured their individual hidden agenda and a little envy, the hosts were delighted to see a man of such obvious importance and asked him to sit with them at the highest table, offering him a plate filled with the choicest delicacies. Then, much to the bewilderment of the hosts and everyone present, Chang removed his coat and turban, placed them before the plate and said, 'Eat, my master, eat.'

'What are you doing?' one of the astonished hosts enquired.

'It is my apparel that you are honouring, not me,' replied Chang.

The conscious, thinking part of each of us that seeks security from an external reality, whether through what we do, who we are, how we appear, or what we have, is fundamentally our ego. Our ego is not a fact, it is an idea; an idea that has pervaded our entire thinking, establishing limitations and boundaries in our beliefs about ourselves. It is an idea that has resulted from perceiving ourselves as a separate individual entity that requires security and protection because it is superior, different or apart from others.

If we consider that Man has two selves, a higher and a lower, the lower is our ego, or more appropriately, our *Earth Guide Officer*. The higher is our actual Self, or more aptly, our *Spiritual Everlasting Loving Friend*. Our lower self is constantly preoccupied with the virtues of its attributes, wanting others to obey moral precepts only as *it* expounds them. Obsessed with presenting itself in ways that gain the good opinion of others, it continually directs a person to pretensions so that people will compliment and praise it. But while praising others in their presence, its tendency is to do the opposite in their absence.

The ego self is the creature born of our own thinking and doing. Forming the sum total of all our memories, habits, opinions and thought patterns, it is a helpful frame of reference and can be a useful tool. But although its services are handy, we have allowed it to become our master rather than our slave, by failing to recognise that its view of how things should be for us only restricts and frustrates us. Considered and often defined as a separate entity, or reality in its own right, it is actually a reflection, albeit extremely limited and distorted, of our higher self.

Our goal must be to allow one to shine through the other, by fulfilling ourselves and learning greater intimacy with our higher self. In this way, we transcend our ego and escape its bondage, so allowing it to be used freely and compassionately with wisdom. When we do not, and continue to be unaware of our ego's false protection, we are only successful in becoming our own worst enemy.

With everyone's attention on him, Chang began to share a story about a wise old sage whom people visited from near and far to seek advice on personal problems.

One day a man awkwardly carrying a large sign struggled up to where the sage lived. His sign read: Here Is A Very Important Person Who Always Knows What He Is Doing.

'The problem I need you to solve,' said the visitor to the sage, 'is how to lighten the terrible weight and irritation that carrying this sign causes me. Please show me how I can do so more comfortably.'

'There is no way, other than the way you currently use,' replied the sage. 'But you can let go of it altogether, although you must have the courage to do so. Yet in so doing you will gain more.'

Not hearing the words of advice he had travelled so far for, the man snapped with hostility, 'But you don't understand, this sign has served me well for many years by attracting money, honour and friends. You cannot begin to imagine how many people believe it simply because they see it. I do not want to think about life without it, as I have become so used to it. I merely want to learn how to keep the sign, while making it more comfortable. It is clear to me, oh wise one,' continued the man sarcastically, 'that you are not as clever as you think you are.' Bidding the sage a cursory good day, he stumbled away with his heavy load.

Concluding his tale, Chang said to those present, 'It is a strange thing that a person is satisfied with so little in himself, but demands so much in others. The emptiest man is the man who is full of himself, for as we all know,' he chuckled, 'the fellow who thinks he is full of knowledge is especially annoying to those of us who are.'

True success in life begins with the subordination of the ego. This means first acknowledging the power that we have allowed our ego to have over us, by recognising its insistent and insatiable demands. Then we must let go of our need to impress others. Such needs generate the insecurities that cause us to put all our efforts into obtaining something perceived as important. It may be a comment that you feel threatens your skill, position or status. It may be the need to have a better car, house, clothes or holiday as a measure of your success in front of other people. Acting as a comfort blanket, our ego influences our decisions with misguided thoughts of security. Thoughts which appear to be in our best interests in the short term, but actually cause us to work against ourselves in the long term.

The difficulty is that, no matter how much we feed the ego, it delivers a new list of demands immediately its previous ones are satisfied. Whatever you give it will never be enough, for it operates in the belief that having more means better security, recognition and importance. And whenever your ego feels your needs are not being met, it demands that you complain about why you are not getting what you should.

The ego wants what it wants immediately, although it does not dwell in the present. Its power is in the past and future, over what should have been, or what ought to happen. Although when satisfied it demands more, when it is unsatisfied it convinces you of how unfair life is and what an awful place the world is. Insecurities increase in direct proportion to the ego's greater control over your life. Thus we look more and more outside of ourselves to fill the emptiness that increasingly grows inside.

Of course, it is hard to be aware that our ego is detrimental to us when it has successfully convinced us that it is protecting us. But when we do become aware of it, and are able to recognise its false demands, it can then be used as an ally rather than a foe. Our ability to regain mastery over our ego requires awareness and understanding of four paradoxical keys: distraction attraction, separated oneness, simplified complexity and fearful love.

Distraction Attraction

'Has Your Majesty never observed the bounding monkeys?' answered Chang to the King of Wei. 'If they can reach the tall cedars, or camphor trees, they will swing and sway from their limbs, frolicking and lording it in their midst, so that even the famous archers Yi or P'eng Meng could not take accurate aim at them. But when they are attracted to what they suppose are delicacies and find themselves among the prickly mulberries, brambles, hawthorns or spiny citrons, way below their loftier arena, they must move with caution, glancing from side to side, quivering and shaking with fear.

'It is not that their bones and sinews have become suddenly stiff and lost their suppleness. It is simply that the monkeys find themselves in a difficult and disadvantageous position, one where they cannot exercise their abilities to the full. And so it is when Man becomes full of himself. His attraction to what is seemingly of benefit and greater security to him, actually distracts him from expressing himself in his full light.'

'I like that tale,' said the King of Wei, 'but knowing you as I do, I have no doubt that the monkey is merely a metaphor for Man's own mischievous self. Our fall from our true identity causes us to improvise and clutch at a false identity with the same desperation as someone falling continuously into the abyss.'

'Exactly so!' said Chang gleefully. 'In the absence of the true knowledge of who we really are, our adopted self must keep alive its fictional existence with convincing, albeit empty, chattering.'

'Chattering which is taken to heart rather than ignored,' said the King. 'Incessant and sweet chattering thoughts that, while sometimes a nuisance, sweetly persuade, convince, cajole, even scare us into believing that if we want protection, security and peace of mind, there is no other self worth listening to.'

'And if such a self was indeed a monkey, how would you, as a sagely King, deal with it?' enquired Chang.

'Why I would ensure that both Yi and P'eng Meng practised harder, until they were successful,' his monarch replied with amusement.

'And how so for your own self, is it also a case of shooting the monkey?' asked Chang.

'Again, I would employ and develop those decisive archer parts of my own being to unmask myself.'

'Well said, my King, for only by such action will you rid yourself of a fictional power that ultimately renders you powerless.'

Both modern psychology and education is based on the idea that, unless a person has a strong ego, he or she cannot succeed in life where there is so much competition. The feeding of the ego, therefore, begins almost immediately, through teaching people, either consciously or unwittingly, not to be the best they can be, but to be better than others. Success is defined by what a person has achieved in comparison to others, rather than in relation to what they themselves are capable of, but have not yet achieved.

Our whole society is geared towards developing the assertive, competitive elements within us, rather than the resolute, co-operative elements. A person will refer to his tutelage of a new recruit, for example, by saying, 'I taught him everything he knows.' In so doing he is maintaining his seniority and position over the pupil. To say, 'I taught him everything I know, and look he has surpassed me with his progress', is too much of a threat to even consider. The actor who receives a lesser billing than his up-and-coming younger protégé, will view them as a Brutus. A recently promoted director will not be comfortable until his appointment is formally announced and he has the office, car, house and expense account that reflect his new position. The importance of these endorsements occupies a person's thinking, distracting them from their new responsibilities. After all, if it is in title only, what will everyone think?

Although elements of the ego are useful as a tool, when the very need to succeed becomes the means and end of what we do, we suffer a kind of implosion. The mushrooming cover that we exude becomes unstable for the stalk that supports it, so that when, not if, we continue to subject ourselves to the notions and whims we deem so important, our world inevitably comes tumbling down.

Doing what is important above what is urgent is obviously the key, but this is not possible without first acknowledging what is important in our life. It is because of the meaningless void in our life that our ego attaches itself to what is considered vital for its survival. Not knowing what is important, our tendency is to drop to the depths of life's numerous distractions, all eager to feed our hungry ego. Receiving praise for a piece of work is a distraction that we allow to take precedent over the work itself. Praise, recognition and being part of accepted society, particularly its élite, are considered more important than the work that we do to express ourselves; reward becomes our motivation.

Reward is certainly a positive motivation in its rightful place, but not when it becomes the sole purpose for what we do. The monkey trained to climb palm trees to retrieve coconuts does so simply for the reward and praise it receives. In a short time the monkey gets bored with what it has to do, however, and begins to refuse. It will not give up its reward, though, as this has become a right. But what of Man? Man's lower self also soon wearies of having to do things that do not interest it yet, similarly, it will not give up its reward. Indeed the ego demands the reward by convincing Man that because of his position and what he does, receiving it is his right. When the reward is no longer forthcoming, for whatever reason, a person will consider its removal as an infringement of personal rights.

Often the ego is interested only in reaping, not sowing. Take the example of two individuals both operating from different perspectives. The first person, a graduate, expects greater rewards than another person who has practical experience but no qualifications. Similarly, the latter person considers his reward should be greater. The former's ego rejects the fact that he has never managed others before, or cannot manage himself; the latter's ego rejects the fact that he lacks understanding of specific managerial skills. Both, however, want the reward that qualifications *and* experience achieve, one because his tutor advised him that he should expect nothing less than management status, the other because he has been there longer.

It is the ego that is in control, seeking the best reward for the least input, rather than seeking reward for being the best of their ability, in due course. Further attractions then follow sequentially, as each is obtained: type of car, size of work-area, position and size of desk, size of expense account, location of office, and so on. Circumstance is irrelevant when external attractions are deemed vitally important to security. Where the sales executive must have air conditioning in the car, the entrepreneur must have another Ferrari.

Our ego causes us to focus in on what we can have, rather than what we can be. It wants you to have without having to do, and to do without having to be. It can devise whatever fictional being, in the form of title or name, it considers is necessary for your protection. Answering the question of what you would have, if you won a million pounds, is easier than answering the question of what you would be. There is of course nothing wrong with ambition, indeed, we must be ambitious to survive, grow and fulfil our potential. But where the human desire to succeed is positive, preoccupation with personal ambition that keeps us constantly wound up, and that measures our success in what we have in comparison to others, is not.

With the focus of our attention meeting the demands of our ego, we insidiously revolve our lives around trivia. Metaphorically attracted by what the monkey is wearing and how it performs, we are distracted from hearing the music that the organ grinder plays for us. This is why so many of us go to our graves with the symphony of our true selves remaining unplayed. Similarly, attracted by the infinite number of toys that we must have to add credence to what we do and what we are, we are consistently distracted from that which we should really occupy ourselves with. History shows that great men and women have lived by the philosophy: 'Whatever anyone thinks of me, is really none of my business.' King Alfred is remembered for ignoring all trivia by burning the cakes; Lord Nelson is remembered for ignoring all trivia by turning a blind eye. Trivia is not detail, it is the whims, notions, suggestions and interferences that both your own ego and those of others insist you pay attention to.

Next time you do something for another, take time to consider why you are doing it; next time you buy something, consider why; next time you seek the credit for something, notice how you feel when you don't get it – threatened, cheated, left out? If you have an expense account do you treat it as if it were your own money? If someone books you into standard rather than business class, do you feel your position or status is threatened? Is what you have and receive in relation to what you do, more important than what you do and give in relation to what you are? Do you think that great people would concern themselves about such things? Are you concerned about what people think of you? Are you allowing your ego to distract you from being great, by being attracted to what society deems is great to have? As one sage said, 'The lower self is like a flame both in its display of beauty and in its hidden potential for destruction; though its colour is attractive, it burns.'

Subordination of the ego requires an awareness of the toys and other attractions that distract us from being our true self, and which we use to decorate our fictional self; attractions that our ego cause us to believe are essential for our protection. This level of awareness can only be developed through involvement with something that is greater than ourselves. Whenever we seek to make a difference in the lives of others through what we do, we begin to control our ego. Those who are controlled by their lower self must serve it; those who control the lower self, serve others. To serve others in such a way that your own success is built on helping the success of others, requires understanding of the second key.

Separated Oneness

Saddened that his only son had run away, a father searched without success. After a few years he chose to settle in a town and, being exceedingly wealthy, he built a fine mansion.

The son, having impulsively attached himself to some travellers after hearing their stories, had in time forgotten all about his home, unaware of his rightful inheritance by birth. Endlessly wandering through foreign lands, the boy soon fell into the habit of just scratching out a living.

There came a time, however, when the son felt drawn back towards his own country, and one day he wandered unknowingly into his father's town and approached the mansion looking for work. Upon seeing the magnificence of the mansion and the greatness of the owner walking the terrace, however, the destitute young man convinced himself that his labour would not be required. So he began to move on. But his father, never forgetting his beloved son's face for one minute, immediately recognised him amongst the crowd outside the gates. Overjoyed he quickly dispatched his most valued retainers to welcome his son home. Noticing the two well-dressed men hurrying towards him, the son unfortunately mistook their intentions. Fearing that he was about to be blamed for something and imprisoned, he fought them off and ran into the slums for refuge.

After hearing what had happened, the father decided upon a different course of action. Sending two more servants, this time dressed in shabby clothes, he instructed them to find his son and offer him, in conversation, some menial labour on the estate. In this way the son started work within his father's mansion. Each day he engaged in his task of clearing an enormous heap of rotting rubbish, returning to the slums each night. In time, becoming more comfortable with his surroundings, the man quit the slums, accepting the use of a humble estate dwelling house. To get closer to him, the father would dress in work clothes, encourage the young man in his work, and invite him to visit the mansion house sometimes.

Working faithfully, his responsibilities increased until in time he became the overseer of the entire estate. But, continuing to feel subservient to his benefactor and unworthy of his generosity, it took more time before the son's diminishing sense of inferiority allowed him to develop a strong and friendly relationship with his father.

The time came when the father felt that his death was approaching. Calling together everyone that was involved with the estate, he announced that the poor man that he had taken in years before and now entrusted with the management of the estate, was in fact his own beloved son to whom all his property now belonged. At last the man was enlightened to the truth, and was amazed at how his earlier delusions had caused him to believe that he was separate from what had been his rightful inheritance.

The father represents our true self, and the son our ego self. The story illustrates how, through choice, we separate ourselves from the whole that makes us one with everything else. Similar to the fall from grace, the eviction from the Garden of Eden, the wandering in foreign lands and the forgetting of our true inheritance, the story symbolises the urge and journey of the human consciousness back towards wholeness. The level of our separateness from all nature as a whole is represented by the extent to which we have wandered into foreign lands, forgotten our birthright and family or connectedness with everything, and live as a destitute, preoccupied with scratching out a living.

By accepting our delusion of being a separate entity, we limit ourselves to what we consider our status quo should be and become preoccupied with seeking external gains to fulfil our habitual needs. But there comes a time in everyone's life when each one of us feels drawn back to a union with what we really are part of. Yet before we can rejoin, there is often an enormous heap of rotting rubbish — delusions, hang-ups, phobias and insecurities — to clear away first. That part of us that recognises our connectedness, allows us to move forward only at the rate that is comfortable for our ego, however long it takes. Forcing progress will have the opposite effect, as the ego is a part of us and cannot be destroyed. It can, however, be subjugated and turned into a servant instead of permitting it to remain a master.

The death of the father, and the son's realisation of his true identity, represent the end of the separation between the true self and the ego self, and the death of self-inferiority. The son is no longer deluded by false limitations. Everything on the journey happened when he was good and ready. He would not have anything forced on him, but by developing faith in himself he was able to take on the management of the whole estate. In other words, he was able to take responsibility for becoming his whole self and acknowledge what it involved.

As the ego lies to itself, to the person who identifies with it, and to others consistently, then training our ego self to accept that its separation is a delusion is challenging. Enlightenment initially involves the realisation that you are at one with everything else. But accepting that the Universe is a complete unit, with nothing divided in it, is unacceptable to the ego. Indeed it shakes the three pillars of separatism: *my, mine* and *I*, the stalwarts of egoism. Egoism is the belief that the organism to which *I* am attached is superior to others, so that *I* measure others by my likes and dislikes, not by their needs; *I* impudently criticise another for making a slip, while being guilty of making bigger blunders. Egoism is *I, I, I*.

The real enemy is not the entity ego, which is part of us, but the function of egoism, which thrives on making us separate and isolated. Egoism is the very glue with which we get stuck to ourselves. It is not about thinking too much of yourself, rather it is about thinking too little of other people. It is about hiding one's misguided sense of inferiority behind the façade of a superiority complex.

Egoism, therefore, causes us to want to control other people, rather than appreciate them; to exploit others on a 'what's in it for me' basis, rather than seek ways to serve them; to be more concerned with competition, rather than direct our focus to co-operation; to seek win:lose situations, rather than develop win:win relationships, to cut a good deal for ourselves, rather than want another to profit as much as we do; to be more concerned with acquiring things, rather than giving of ourselves; to increase our ownership of goods, rather than being willing to share with others; and to be more focused on our personal self, rather than our universal self.

The truth however, is that the less self-centred we learn to become, the more we are in tune with others and can enjoy our universal inheritance. When we begin to accept that there are other beliefs, we embark on the journey towards the realisation that we are not separate entities, but are all one. This great truth of oneness is the ultimate experience, because our conscious realisation of it removes the limitations that we have allowed ourselves to have in every area of our lives.

Everything in the Universe operates under the same metaphysical laws. But the prime force behind those laws is a Universal Spirit of Infinite Life, Power and Intelligence. Throughout the world, numerous names exist, but they all refer to the Spiritual Force known as God. Similar to the varying sizes of ocean waves that in their real form are all water, each of us is an individualised spirit which does not differ in essence from the Infinite Spirit that we are part of. It follows that our individualised powers are potentially without limitation, because we are connected to their very source. Indeed, the only limitations we have are the very same ones we set ourselves, by virtue of believing we are separate entities. Comparing ourselves with others, either feeling superior or inferior, therefore, is as absurd as the small wave that compares itself with a large wave.

When we hear such aphorisms as, 'the only things we never lose are the things we give away', they affect us in such a way as to know that they are true. Yet our ego does not want us to reflect on such thoughts, as they undermine the belief that we are separate and need to be protected. It immediately replaces them, therefore, with thoughts such as, 'we deserve more than we have, and anything we give away we will have to do without.' In doing so it re-establishes its control over us, refocusing our mind as to what we need to maintain our security. 'Giving to get' is an inescapable law of the ego, which always evaluates itself in relation to other egos. It is therefore continually preoccupied with the belief in scarcity that gave rise to it. The ego literally lives by comparisons and equality is beyond its grasp.

Metaphysically each of us is constantly drawing to us the conditions that fit our dominant thoughts. That is why it is so vitally important to keep our minds on what we want, rather than on what we don't want. Our conditioned difficulty is clearly that, even that which we think we want will not be in our long-term best interests if the desire has originated from egotistical thinking. Whenever we strive to acquire that which we believe protects us, we are actually strengthening the ego and weakening our inheritance.

Personal Labels

From the cutting of the umbilical cord our quest to discover who we are commences. As a child we begin to possess; we think, this toy is *mine*, this mother is *mine*. Possessiveness is very basic, which is why all scriptures uniformly advise becoming non-possessive, as with possession, hell starts. Small children jealously and possessively guard their toys, while trying to snatch everything from everyone else. Some children will fiercely cling to a toy, ready to hit and fight if necessary over any infringement of their territory and domination.

Once the idea of *mine* exists you are a competitor with everybody, embarking on a journey of struggle, conflict, violence and aggression. The next step is *me*. Having something to claim generates the beginning of the idea that you are the centre of your possessions. Like the spider in the centre of its web, possessions become your territory, a personal universe from which arises the idea of *me*.

Labelling yourself '*me*' defines a boundary. This is where things start to go wrong, as you rely on defined ego boundaries to separate yourself from others. From the reflection of *me* within these boundaries arises *I*, the subtlest and most crystallised form of possessiveness. The *I* cannot relax, as it exists through tensions, creating new worries, concerns and fears. But the *I* we create emanates from a false centre. At the real centre, the whole existence is one, just as all the sun's rays emanate from one source of light.

A false centre and identity is manufactured because without boundaries we would be unable to compartmentalise who we are, something that society insists that we do. Our tendency when meeting others, for example, is to immediately seek to get a handle on them by labelling them for what they do, or have done. Unless we can label or compartmentalise them according to our own frame of reference, they make us uncomfortable. We may even perceive them as a threat. So, given a name and some idea of who we are by others, we gather the things people say about us and develop a certain image.

Somebody says we are beautiful, another says we are intelligent, another says we are important. But as our inner reality is not available to anyone except ourselves, the image is going to be false. The ideas that we gather from others may give us personality, but the knowledge we come to know through understanding our true selves gives us individuality, an authenticity that can never be borrowed, unlike personality.

Even though we have been taught for centuries to 'know thyself', we never really listen. Too intent on being the person we pretend to be to bother about it, we go on clinging to anything from the outside that may assure us of who we are. The fact is that no-one, other than you, can say who you are.

But how we develop *is* part of a process, a process that involves losing one's self, before we can regain it. The infant without its ego boundaries may be in closer touch with reality than its parents, but it is incapable of surviving without their care. And it is incapable of communicating its wisdom. Ego boundaries have to be hardened before they can be softened, and an identity, however false, must be established before it can be transcended.

Often it is our growing awareness of our own mortality that causes us to seek the path of knowing ourselves. The death of a close friend, or the ending of a particular cycle in our lives, a metaphorical death in itself, is often the catalyst for wanting to understand our own spirituality. Perhaps the best idealist must first be a materialist, as it is easier to give up something you have first acquired or experienced.

Increasingly, people are seeking greater meaning and purpose in their lives. Perhaps, having settled on the shore of what was believed to be the land of fulfilment, we are discovering that it is not as fruitful as we had thought. As if recognising that the sight of one shore must disappear before an alternative can be sighted, people are embarking on their own particular spiritual journey, a voyage that must pass through what is seemingly a sea of emptiness before their destination is reached. The Western world is gradually choosing sustainable quality over disposable quantity; businesses are seeking to develop the co-operation essential to serve mutual customers; people are becoming more aware that the key is to think *we, us* and *ours.* There is clearly an increasing wave of consciousness embracing the understanding of oneness and accepting the responsibilities in moving from egotistical separation towards oneness. To recognise the separateness of the ego is the first step, to discern the falsity and absurdity of the movements of egoism is the second; to discourage and refuse it at each step is the third. But it can only be completely subjugated when one sees, experiences and acknowledges that everything is equally connected everywhere. Lasting enlightenment, or true spiritual growth, such as this, can only be achieved through the persistent exercise of real compassion for creation as a whole, including one's fellow beings.

Simplified Complexity

An Emperor was travelling the country with his enormous entourage of courtiers and advisors, when he came upon a remote village that he had not visited before. The custom of the countryside was such that people would always offer an Emperor their very best. But the villagers had nothing of value to offer, so they sent their elders to the Emperor to tell him, 'We have something precious to offer you that was handed down by our ancestors.'

Seeing nothing in their hands, the Emperor asked, 'What is it?'

The spokesman for the elders stepped forward and replied, 'In the wintertime, if you sit in the sunshine you will feel very comfortable.'

Bemused by their answer the Emperor began to laugh, as did the whole entourage. 'Everyone knows that, it is no secret,' he said, 'but I accept your simple yet "precious" gift.'

Returning home, the Emperor reflected on the words of the village elders. 'Life is simple yet man makes it complex,' he thought. 'As an Emperor I can have anything I want, yet the more I have, the more complicated my life becomes. My life is more a reflection of what others expect an Emperor to be, rather than how I truly am. Their reflection has become my reality. I do what I do because I am expected to, because I am able to, yet it seems that there is little time to just live.'

The ego will cling fiercely to whatever false and complex structure it deems essential for our security. Indeed, it welcomes complexity above all else, as it considers that greater complexity means more challenging stimulation. Thus, there is a tendency within our personal and professional lives to complicate rather than simplify things. Despite the fact that waste thrives on complexity, most businesses engage in it, generating prodigious amounts of needless, unproductive and expensive activity. The greater the sense of importance attached to being involved with what is complex, the greater the activity and the less the productivity.

In a material-focused world, where success means having more, activity is mistaken for productivity. Consequently, activities are focused on that which brings about greater importance and complexity, because they will bring the rewards and recognition that are seen to be necessary for a person's protection. In reality, because the ego is only concerned with illusory protection, nothing lasts, and the more a person feels they have to protect, the more insecure they feel.

*   *   *

Sage Yang-Chu once said to his Emperor, 'People will always be active in seeking satisfaction in good food, fine clothes, lively music and sexual pleasure. Many will in time realise that meeting their material needs does not create the happiness hoped for. So society becomes active in setting up reward systems that go beyond material goods.'

'You refer to such things as titles, social recognition, status, and political, bureaucratic and organisational power,' said the Emperor, 'all wrapped up in a package called self-fulfilment.'

'Exactly so,' said Yang-Chu. 'Attracted by such prizes and goaded by social pressure, people spend their lives actively chasing after these goals, feeling that they have achieved something. But the reality is that they have sacrificed a lot in their life because they can no longer productively see, hear, act, feel or think from their hearts. Everything they do is dictated by whether it leads to social gain. In the end, they've spent their lives following the demands of others, never living their own life.'

'Then they might just as well be living the life of a slave or prisoner.'

'Just so, and many unwittingly do,' continued Yang-Chu. 'The ancients understood that life is only a temporary sojourn in this world, and death is a temporary leave. In our short time here, we should listen to our voices and follow our hearts. Why follow other people's rules and live to please others? Is it not better to be free and live your own life, enjoying whatever comes your way to the full?'

'It is so,' said the Emperor. 'For being imprisoned by name or title allows social conventions to lead one away from the natural order of things.'

'Certainly, and concern over whether one is remembered in generations ahead is a wasteful activity, as our present consciousness will not be there to see it. Rather than spend their life letting other people manipulate them just to get a name and a reputation, a person must let their life be guided by their own heart.'

'So one must live without the burdens of fame and recognition,' said the Emperor.

'One must simply live without the self-importance that requires their necessity. For self-importance devises complexity to sustain itself, which runs *against the simple and natural order of things. Thus, the more a person feels they must have, the more they feel they must protect what they have. So, unwittingly, they build a prison maze around themselves, one so complex that keys to get out of it are unnecessary.'*

'Then how is it possible for a person to regain their freedom?' asked the Emperor.

'By the only means to see one's bondage for what it really is,' answered Yang-Chu. 'Simply to rise above it.'

Having convinced us that we are much less than we really are, the ego measures our value by what our 'busyness' accomplishes. We have become so tied up with what we do, for example, that we view weekends or time off as our periodical escape. Yet the complexity of our lives is such that these escapes only lead to the exercise yard of our self-imposed prison. Could we but rise above all the complications in our lives and see that they have been created to satisfy the demands of ego, we would know the absurdity of what reassuring it continually requires of us. Do we really need the security blanket of electronic luggage to verify our identity? Do we allow the tools and toys of our particular profession to simplify our lives, as they were intended to? Do we need the complexity of systems to ensure that our business runs smoothly? Do we need the complexity that we create in our relationships? Must we really have the complexity we have in our lives in order to live? Or is it simply that we have allowed ourselves to be convinced that we do? Think how much more energy we use trying to get around something, rather than just getting on with it. In doing so, we complicate the issue.

Complexity is born out of a belief that things cannot be simple. Seeking to reduce the complexity of whatever stressful concern you may currently have, will initially cause your ego to ridicule you by saying, 'Ah, but that's easier said than done.' No, it isn't. Try it. Allow yourself to become aware of something being unnecessarily complex. Feel what would be the clearest and simplest solution. Again your ego will say, 'But that's too obvious to work.' Then just do it, and importantly, be aware of how easy it is. If something sounds right to you, because deep down inside it *feels* right to you, then do it. Act on it.

If something goes against the grain, however, dismiss it. But in doing so be aware of why you are dismissing it. To dismiss something is fine, but to not know why you do so allows the ego to say, 'Go on, convince me.' Whatever is true does not need to be defended, it only has to be remembered. Whenever something *feels* right, it is because you already know it to be right. Acting in this manner allows you to simplify your life. We complicate things more out of fear than anything else. Fear, the ego's main tool leads us to the key to overcoming it.

Fearful Love

As the world equates business and career success with personal success and honours the wealthy and accomplished, the fear of failure is one of the most common and powerful forces in the workplace. When things are going well for us, we do not believe they will last. So rather than simply monitor what we are doing, we begin to complicate things in the belief that, without our increased active interference, our success will not continue. Inevitably, because of our interference, we bring about what we are afraid of.

For example, two people of equal ability embark on separate transactions. Both do all that is necessary for them and to the best of their abilities. One, however, perceives the outcome of their transaction as vital, in terms of income, recognition and self-esteem. The other has no such attachments and, having done all that is possible, begins to think about the next transaction. While the latter monitors progress, the former interferes, tweaking things here and there. The paradox of success is that the harder you push for something, the further it will move in the other direction. The person who pushes the chain has no control over the links, and they travel in all directions. The person in control is the person who pulls the chain straight. This principle also applies to the leadership of people. Pushing people to do what your ego considers they ought to do is not as effective as them following you, compelled to by your example.

All fears, including the fear of failure and the fear of success, are misguided beliefs that rob us of our peace of mind and upset our lives, spawned by the ego which wants us to forget our own inherent self-worth. We have forgotten that we are divine beings, created to perform the exact opposite of fear and so with the power to miraculously transform all difficult situations we encounter. Creating the exact opposite of fear is aligned to our true self, that higher, *Spiritual Everlasting Loving Friend* that guides us towards fulfilment of our purpose. And what is the exact opposite of fear? It is certainly not courage, although it takes courage to apply it. It is the compassion one feels for one's fellow beings, the very substance that makes our lives worth living — it is love.

The word love conjures up different meanings for people. When sincerely meant, 'I love you' is, for many, one of the hardest things to say. In those few words we open ourselves up to share something with another that leaves us vulnerable. Mentioning such a word in the business arena, apart from in the context of 'I love my work', is simply not appropriate, considered the worst of all that is associated with that 'touchy feely stuff'. That is because, in not understanding what *true* love involves, we have allowed our egos to compartmentalise it into something that is just not done in public.

Where fear is about closing ourselves up, love is about opening ourselves up. But in the world of business particularly, we have learned to fear the very opposite of what keeps us in our status quo. Indeed, in all situations we seem to prefer to fear love, sticking instead to that which is more familiar to us. Thus, we take more than we give in the belief that giving means to sacrifice and lose something. The world tells us that what we have is diminished if we give, yet to receive more we must give more, and the best thing we can learn to give is love. But the love we must learn to give is not the love that we generally associate with the word, the limited or conditional love we habitually extend to a particular person or thing. It is a divine and unconditional love that reaches beyond what is familiar to us.

Our very reason for being is the learning and teaching of unconditional love. For it is only through love that we can truly grow. It is what we were created for and is the path essential for fulfilling our potential. But loving our unfamiliar neighbour does not mean that we open ourselves up to abuse from them. It does not mean having to like them, or to put up with inadequate work or disrespectful behaviour from them, as our ego will immediately suggest. It is therefore important to understand what is meant by unconditional love.

Most of us have experienced the meaning of unconditional love, if only for a fleeting moment. At the moment of an offspring's birth, a parent will feel unconditional love. A father holding his son for the first time is filled with an overwhelming sense of joy. Fascinated by his child's vulnerability and dependency he promises to do everything necessary to give him a good life. He will obviously not consider a contract of conditional love, whereby he will look after him *only* on the condition that he receives love, appreciation and gratitude in return. Yet a form of conditional love soon begins within the relationship.

The father may even make his son feel guilty for the father himself not having fulfilled his own promise to his son. In time the father and son may hardly meet each other lovingly. The son goes to the father when he needs money and the father goes to the son when he wants to give a sermon. Loving conditionally, the father becomes increasingly afraid of interaction.

It is because we are only prepared to love according to conditions that we are afraid of falling in love. As frightened people, we seek to make everything secure, according to our ego's conditions, looking for those things which our loved ones wouldn't do if they really loved us. Is it any wonder, therefore, that we consider it almost impossible to love whatever is uncomfortable or beyond what is familiar to us? 'Love your neighbours as your *self*' isn't allowed a moment's thought, let alone 'love your enemies'.

The only way to love your neighbour as your own self is to see your own self in that person. That follows our prime purpose of self-discovery, for it is not possible to see your self in another if you don't know your self. In so doing there can be no enemies. Since love is our true nature, our inheritance from our Creator whose nature is also love, the way to self-discovery is to learn and teach unconditional love. For in doing so, we begin to remember who we really are.

As the best way to learn something is to teach it, the best way to learn love is to teach love. This validates the truism that the only way to receive love is to give love. Learning to love unconditionally creates miracles, for any miracle is simply an act of unconditional love. All of us are given the opportunity to create miracles in our lives, every hour and every day, simply through treating others as we ourselves would want to be treated. We don't always take the time to do so, but when we do we are treating others unconditionally. In doing so, we also clarify our own thinking because we have dispersed our own fears.

Choosing to love and forgive another who has offended us,

is acknowledging that they are also learning like us. It may be that we have to dismiss another, divorce another, terminate a situation or take legal action against another. But in doing so from love, rather than judgement, we end the personal pain and stress that such action and conflict has previously put us through. It is not possible to predict what miracle will come about from our acting out of love rather than anger towards another.

The offending person may change, or not, but when love has been allowed to enter the situation, things do happen. It may be that acting through love towards someone we previously resented and judged, results in our physical removal from them due to a miraculous change in circumstances. They, or we, may be transferred or choose another job. What happens to resolve our difficult situation is later viewed as a wonderful set of beneficial coincidences.

Introducing love into a problematic situation is about reducing the fear within ourselves, not learning to love someone we do not even like. Everyone benefits when we release our fears and are able to live more in peace with ourselves. When a person says that they love one person but hate another, they do not know what love is. For love is not limited, it is divine and unlimited. When we respond from love, we respond from our true nature and allow our Divine Will, not our human will, to affect the results. In doing so we harness the most powerful force in the Universe. One that always offers peace, instead of conflict.

There may be someone currently in your life that is causing you difficulty. It may be someone who always seems to make things difficult for you on purpose, either personally or professionally. Begin to think of them with love, forgiving them for their behaviour and actions towards you. This is admittedly difficult because you have to send loving thoughts, rather than vengeful, aggressive ones. But know that despite the unjustness of the way in which they are acting towards you, their actions are based on their own insecurities. Accept that they are acting the way they do because they are afraid, frightened, insecure and isolated. They are merely operating from an ego that has convinced them that you are a threat, and must be put under their control.

When you actively do this, you will soon sense a strength within you that you did not feel before. You will know that you will overcome whatever difficulty they present without allowing it to affect you. In this way, you take charge of how things will turn out. In due course, the situation will resolve itself in a way that you had not previously imagined. This does require courage, but the only way you will resolve your fears is through addressing them with love, unconditionally. Our ego self acts through fear, our true Self, acts through love. When people bring up your flaws, you resent them for it; but when a good mirror reflects your ugliness, you consider it to be a good mirror. Learning to deal with others without involving your ego, will always prevent you being dragged down by them.

Quantum Improvement

Freedom from the ego involves being aware of the continuous attractions it puts in front of us – external desires that serve only to distract us from being our true Self. It means resolving to regain our natural inheritance through acknowledging that there is a source of oneness that we all emanate from. It means reducing the complexity of our life, removing the trivia that we have allowed to insidiously fill our life, under the misguided belief that it is fulfilling. It means accepting that our primary purpose is to learn, and teach, an unconditional love. It means understanding that no-one is in our life by accident, that they provide opportunities for us to grow into our true Self.

How we express ourselves, through the work which we

choose to do, is by far the best arena to develop ourselves, because business brings out the worst expression of the ego. It does so because it involves what we earn, our credibility, our position in society, our social standing, our esteem, and above all, our fears and insecurities. All elements of the workplace offer great opportunity for the ego to fully express itself. The culture of a business, whether a small company or large organisation, is the manifestation of how people think and feel, thoughts and feelings emanating from egos.

The greater the level of control for control's sake within the members of a company the smaller their level of self-confidence and self-esteem. When the former goes up the latter goes down, and all other factors, including interpersonal communication, credit-seeking and vying for position are influenced accordingly. Fortunes continue to be spent on change programmes in order to improve culture and alter 'the way things are around here'. Most, however, never consider the greatest source from which insecurities, cynicism, scepticism and other impediments emanate.

Seeking to gain freedom from the ego through recognising its detrimental influence and regaining mastery over it, thus harnessing it as a useful tool, will cause a quantum improvement in how the evolving organisation operates. Addressing the ego will dramatically maximise returns and minimise overheads, while at the same time developing rock-solid customer and client relationships. Like any continuous improvement initiative its process is never ending, but the benefits are priceless to everyone involved, both measurably and immeasurably.

Such a quantum improvement will mark the difference between those individuals who work for the sake of themselves and those who work for the sake of others. The belief that business is different from life in general is a myth. Doing unto others before they do it to you, and treating the person behind the desk differently from the customer in front of the desk, is no longer sustainable. Is it any wonder that the majority of businesses do not reach maturity? In the evolving business arena, those leaders who are influenced and driven by the limited and restrictive beliefs of the ego, will not bear fruit as abundantly as those leaders who have mastery over the ego, free from all limited and restrictive thinking.

In the evolving business arena the difference between the two alternatives is becoming increasingly noticeable. Being yourself and gaining whatever you want through building your success on the success of others follows the natural order of things. Getting whatever you want through building your success on the backs of others does not.

The Chinese monkeys who have philosophically seen no evil, heard no evil and spoken no evil for centuries, are a good example of how to master what is detrimental to us. It is the mischievous and chattering ego within us, however, that we must also free ourselves from in order to embrace the new business spirit so essential for success and meaning. When we become aware of perceiving it, of how we listen to it and how we give it voice, it is actually in our interest to shoot, metaphorically speaking, the monkey within us. The leaders, achievers, the new 'Greats', who do so, will be taking a quantum leap in both their personal and professional lives.

The Eighth Scroll: Guiding the Horse

The Secret of Governing Your Power of Constancy

馬

The horse reared in fright as the shrouded man walked unexpectedly on to the path and startled it.

'Ho there,' cried the carriage driver, struggling to regain control of his animal. 'What devil does such a thing! What do you think you are doing suddenly appearing like that?'

'In peace, I am no devil, moreover, if there were a demon it is within your hand, creating a reign of terror over unsuspecting travellers,' answered the man.

'You are either a sage or a simpleton, speaking as you do,' said the carriage driver. 'The former, I'll wager, for any fool can see that this powerful horse has been finely trained and is well harnessed.'

'Of what good is the strength of a horse and the control of a harness, if the direction of the will guiding the driver's hand is elsewhere?' said the sage. 'It is clear that you are on this road against your will.'

'What nonsense do you speak of?' retorted the carriage driver, wondering how the sage had hit upon the truth with his last remark. 'Explain yourself, or you'll feel the lash of more than my tongue!'

'The fine carriage in which you sit can be likened to the body; the powerful horse to your feelings and desires; you, as driver, are like the mind; and your will is the master of them all. Will is the development of a wish, the command

that turns a wish into action. It is clear that you have no wish to travel wherever you now go, because your will was not ready for the unexpected. The unexpected is the test of true constancy, Man's self-governing key. You did not wish this trip, so your will lacked the tenacity, steadfastness, stability and fortitude that a road such as this demands. A resolute will has power, control and direction working together. When Man lacks this unity, his lack of will is plain for all to see, no matter how he may disguise it.'

'In truth, I have no desire to make this trip,' said the carriage driver. 'But the will of my master is such that I have no choice, though in my heart I know misfortune will come of the business I am ordered to do.'

'It is indeed far easier to train a wild beast than to educate one's own will to perform, because of Man's uncertainty as to what he really wants,' replied the sage. 'That is why Man continues to yield the power of his own will to the will of others and calls it destiny.'

Our will is the greatest power available to us and the very element that determines our success or failure. Will is the basis of our power of constancy, the virtue that encapsulates our tenacity, steadfastness, determination, resolution, perseverance and fortitude; the basis of our zeal, faithfulness and devotion to that which is important to us. The education and formation of our will plays a much more important role in our success, or failure, than the education and formation of our intellect. Yet, amazingly, the development of our will is left to merciless chance.

The reason that one person succeeds to every ten that fail in business is because the factors that are necessary for the development of an indomitable will are not recognised, understood or applied. Our whole education system is based on developing the brain in proportion to the amount of intelligent exercise and use to which it is put. But the education that is overlooked is the strength of constancy and will necessary for life's path. The person who has education, qualifications, rank and position, yet lacks constancy, lacks a great deal in life. The person who lacks money may miss out on certain things in life, but the person who lacks the power of will misses everything in life.

There is inevitably more chance of falling than of rising in life. Few devote their attention to the cultivation of will, and since we have not been taught how to use it, most of us do not know. Consequently, we float along where the current of the will of others takes us, our own submerged, or drowned, from lack of use.

Unwittingly, in our logical thinking, we divide consciousness from will. In the East consciousness *means* will, and the same word is used for will and freedom. By unconsciously giving up our will, we are effectively giving up our freedom. Destiny is always at work with free will, and free will with destiny. They are one and the same thing; the difference is one of consciousness. The more we become conscious of our will, the more we see that destiny works around it and that destiny works according to it. The less conscious we are of that will, the more we see ourselves as subject to destiny.

People generally choose to believe in either destiny or free will. Often it is a question of temperament and the experience they have had in their lives. Some people have worked, had success and recognised it as the outcome of their work. Others, having worked and not succeeded, believe that there is something holding them back which must be destiny. But whether we believe in destiny or not, all of us are attracted to knowing more about it, because seeing what the future holds for us is the greatest desire of all.

Each of us is born with a plan to be accomplished in life, together with the talents, strengths and instinctive abilities to achieve it. Each of us is attached to a divine plan, yet we all have the free will to create our own individual plan and thus continually change our destiny. There are, therefore, two aspects of will working through all things in life — an unconscious will and a conscious will. When our free will and the Divine Will work together, things go smoothly; when they are at odds it is like swimming against the tide.

Developing the indomitable will available to us requires us to tap into the energy that fuels all we are capable of achieving and infinitely more. It is the power that turns wishes into reality. But to do so effectively it must have three attributes working together. It must have strength, be under control and be properly directed. A weak will won't get you far if it is not properly directed; a strong will that is not under control is like a horse without a harness, powerful but unfit for pulling. And the strong will that lacks proper direction is like the carriage horse reined by a half-hearted driver.

Will is the guide that must master itself, as it is the very power of our self-direction and the strongest expression of the life force within each of us. The human will is as much a living force of nature as is gravity, magnetism or electricity. Learning to cultivate and guide such a force changes the individual from mediocre to outstanding. To do so requires both education and application of determined willingness, disciplined perseverance and decisive intent. These three keys are the basis of developing the power of constancy and self-government.

Determined Willingness

'What if they say no? If only I didn't have to worry so much about things. Why can't life be more generous?'

'It can, Han Yen,' said Yun Chu, overhearing his nephew talking to himself. 'You simply have to be determined about what you ask for and be willing to sacrifice in order to receive.'

'Sacrifice what?' said Han Yen. 'I don't have anything to sacrifice.'

'Your own will always find a way, for it is the very functionary of your wishes and knows what to sacrifice when necessary,' began Yun Chu. 'But when you have many desires, which are only the primitive stage of wishes, your mind is scattered and your will deteriorates. Only when your desire becomes a firm and definite wish can it be developed by your will. But you have to know what you want, or your will may deliver to you that which you did not expect.

'There was once a man, for instance, who deep in thought about how he could improve his lot, walked into the jungle. Becoming tired, he found a beautiful tree and sat beneath it. But he couldn't lie down anywhere because the ground was so thorny. "How nice it would be if I had a bed to rest on," thought the man, and no sooner had he done so than he found himself lying down on one. "Yi! This is magnificent. A very comfortable bed to rest on, but I am so hungry I could eat anything. Certainly a banana would be nice." Immediately a bunch of bananas appeared.

'"What's this? I can't believe my eyes. It seems that whatever I want, I get here. Right then, how about some gourmet cooking?" Immediately, plates filled with choice delicacies appeared. Eating sumptuously the man thought, "Ah, how nice it would be for someone to massage my tired feet so that I could fall asleep." Even as he thought of it, there was already a beautiful angel massaging his feet. Now really excited, the man thought, "By the gods this is fantastic! Whatever I'm thinking, I'm getting. Now I have a comfortable bed, a good sumptuous meal and somebody to massage my feet. But what if, while I'm getting the massage, I fall asleep and suddenly a tiger comes from the jungle. What will happen?" Immediately he heard the roar, and a tiger appeared and devoured him.'

'How crazy to have found such a gift and wasted it so!' said the story-teller's nephew.

'Exactly so,' said Yun Chu, 'but such is the thinking of many. Despite walking into the jungle thinking about what he wanted, his will lacked constancy and soon began to desire just basic comforts. If you were to find the fabled boon-giving tree that is ready to give you anything, what would you ask? It

*won't give it to you until you ask and if you ask for bitter fruit, that will
be your destiny.'*

*'But I would only ask for that which I knew would be in my best
interests,' protested Han Yen.*

*'Ah nephew,' said Yun Chu, 'but what are they? For your earlier thoughts,
even spoken out loud to strengthen them, were about worry.'*

Often the meaning of fables is lost. The boon-giving tree, that
place to go, think what you want and get it, has been transformed
over the centuries into the Christmas tree, a once-a-year tree with
all the gifts underneath. Somehow, our thinking has evolved the
view that we should not ask for things, or expect what we want
to be given to us. Not choosing to look beyond the meaning of
'ask and you will receive', we hope for the best, while expecting
the worst.

Having determination for something is of no use on its own.
Neither is perseverance, nor personal drive. These concepts are
not the keys to bring what we want into reality. The cries of,
'I really gave it everything I had' or 'Even after persevering for
ages, nothing happened' and 'Never mind, you did the best
you could have done', may all have determination, perseverance
and personal drive behind them. But there is still something
lacking from the state of mind necessary to bring about what
is wanted. That key factor is for us to be *willing* to do whatever
is necessary.

Whenever a person resolutely determines something and is
truly willing to do what is necessary, regardless of obstacles, the
indomitable will becomes active. Whatever is asked in such a
way is received, for absolutely nothing can resist a willing faith.
That willing faith is the boon-giving tree, and each of us holds
the roots of it within us. What is required is to feel strongly
enough about what we want, in order that willing branches can
bear fruit. Being willing is a measure of the rightness of your

wish or dream. How much something feels right to you, is in direct proportion to how willing you feel about working towards it. Whenever you feel unwilling about what you think is right for you, it is a clear indication that it is not.

Being willing to work eight hours a day on achieving something which requires a willingness of eighteen hours a day, for example, is not about doing what it takes. But the amazing thing about willingness is that holding the thought is often enough. Paradoxically, it does not require greater effort, for the power of will is such that, if one has sufficient willingness, one can find anything one wants to find. Like the stories of archaeologists, historians, researchers and scientists, all of whom hold an uncompromising willingness, who come across what they are looking for almost as soon as they start looking. In other words, they are guided towards it. It is the same with the poet, the musician, the thinker. When they are deeply interested in what they are doing, then they only have to wish, and by the automatic action of their wish – the will – what they want comes to light.

Similarly, willing business entrepreneurs will streak ahead of other leading organisations in an industry, because their will has made possible that which was considered impossible. When both free will and Divine Will, usually unstuck by half-heartedness, become fused by your willingness, providence literally guides you towards your objective.

Determined willingness is providence itself and is harnessed simply through a certainty that what you want is in harmony with your conviction. Individuals with determined willingness do not acknowledge what others refer to as bad luck. But as ninety-nine out of every one hundred people are never clear as to what they really wish, it is not possible for them to either develop determination or willingness. Development of both attributes comes when you are clear about what you desire, so that the powerful will, the controlled will and the directional will work in unison to manifest the object of your desire.

Of the remaining ninety-nine people who are undecided about their desires, some analyse them until they are destroyed; some adopt a passive attitude based on the belief that it is a sin to desire; some hold desires but lack the determination to turn them into a wish, the undeveloped state of will, thus keeping their desires in their primitive stage; and some turn their desires into firm wishes and act on them, but only for the time they perceive it *should* take, thus being unwilling to do whatever it takes.

The reality of life is that absolutely no-one can exist in the world without wishing for something. Man is great or small, wise or foolish, on the right or wrong road, according to the desire he has. What makes a strong or weak will is a greater or lesser permanence of desires and wishes. It is fundamentally crucial, therefore, to do whatever it takes to discover what it is we really wish to do with full willingness. If not, knowing that there is more we can do, mediocrity and frustration will always follow us. Daily practice of recognising what you are both willing and determined enough to see through is required, and this leads us to the second key.

Disciplined Perseverance

Passing through a forest on his way back from Ch'u, a Patriarch saw a hunchback catching cicadas with a sticky pole.

'What skill you have,' he exclaimed. 'How you seize those elusive flying insects as easily as though grabbing them with your hand! What special way have you learned to do such a thing?'

'I have a way,' replied the hunchback. 'For the first five or six months I practise balancing two balls on top of each other at the end of the pole and,

*if they don't fall off, I know I will lose very few cicadas. Then I balance
three balls and, if they don't fall off, I know I'll lose only one cicada in ten.
Then I balance five balls and, if they don't fall off, I know it will be as easy
as grabbing them with my hand. I hold my body like a stiff tree trunk and use
my arm like an old dry limb. No matter how huge heaven and earth, or how
numerous the ten thousand things, I'm aware of nothing but cicada wings. So,
how can I help but succeed?'*

*The Patriarch turned to his disciples and said, 'See how a Man's spirit
concentrated through disciplined perseverance keeps his will undivided. Such
power of constancy makes even the impossible look easy!'*

We are all capable of persisting. Each of us has displayed our
natural ability to steadfastly persist when taking our first step.
Learning to walk takes courage, determination, self-discipline
and perseverance. Yet for too many these natural attributes
disappear from lack of use. The 'do I have to' and 'can't
someone else do that' syndrome is soon born, strengthened
by the appeasement of others.

Winners are people who work at doing things that the
majority of people are not willing to do. Not being willing to
do something, does not mean not being able to do something.
Every day there are incredible success stories of individuals
who, seemingly unable to be or do, because of disability,
adversity, or poverty, overcome all. They win through because
their willingness has developed the discipline and persistence
to do so.

Without discipline the will still exists. However, in its
uncontrolled state it operates as wilfulness, a stubbornness
exerted when one is not willing to do something that one
is capable of doing. Wilfulness is unchannelled will-power,
undisciplined will. When we do not develop the discipline
to harness it, then it works against us, although we may not
be aware of it. Like the stubborn horse that will not be guided

away from the path of an oncoming train because it has not finished a tasty morsel growing on the track, our wilfulness can also cause us to be run over. Often wilfulness is more noticeable in the very young, or very old, because the channel to direct it is lacking. A child will insist that a drink stays precariously on the edge of a table; an aged person will insist that certain possessions are zealously kept in place.

But as discipline is a very personal factor, many people lack persistence; they are only willing to do just what is necessary. That is why we marvel at those individuals who do succeed, but rather than acknowledge the years of discipline and persistence it has taken them, our tendency is to give credit elsewhere. Thus, the outstanding athlete is *extra* talented; the successful person in business had *extra* support, backing, luck or ruthlessness; the talented musician plays an *extra* good quality instrument; and so on. People will always seek to find another reason for not accepting that they themselves lack discipline and persistence. The fact is, however, that our characters and potential can never reach their best until they are rechannelled with these natural attributes.

Developing discipline means choosing to be firm with yourself until what you are undertaking becomes a habit. Thus, rising an hour earlier to train in, study or work at something that you have promised yourself you will do until it is complete, is discipline. If what you are doing requires early rising for years and you stick at it for just weeks or months, then what you are involved with is of only temporary interest to you, a fad. Developing perseverance does not mean sticking to the same thing for ever, but it does mean going through the trials and errors of what you want to achieve. It means giving full concentration and effort to the moment. It means doing the hard things first and finishing them before the easy things. It means going that extra mile to achieve what is important to you.

Where discipline maintains the habit to do what you have undertaken, perseverance sustains the strength of the habit. Habitually practising whatever you are willing to be or do, with the enjoined quality of disciplined perseverance, is the vital ingredient that has developed every past, present or future champion.

The evolving business world increasingly demands that individuals embark on what they do with discipline, accepting such a way as a personal responsibility. This is, of course, how things should be, but is not so in reality. Most discipline is used by one person to control another for obedience purposes, rather than for developing constancy within the individual. With constancy, external obedience is not necessary, as people recognise the importance and observe the power of how individual wills can work together for common purpose.

To develop such discipline first requires matching the right talents and strengths with the appropriate responsibilities. Making others do something that they are clearly unwilling to do is setting discipline against stubbornness, which is not in the interest of our family, group, team or company. Obviously you have to be sure that the stubbornness is not in fact laziness, but strengthening round wheels with square pegs is a measure that will ultimately distort the wheel and make the ride rough for everyone. As our natural tendency is to do whatever is easiest first, then procrastinate over what is clearly the hardest method, it is obviously best to focus high priority work on the most productive areas which will further develop disciplined perseverance.

When we are choosing of our own volition to persist in doing more than we are asked and contribute more than is required, we become able to expect the unexpected. When we come to expect the unexpected we are ready for anything. Confident in the strength of our discipline we remain unconcerned, irrespective of what we may have to suddenly deal with.

With our persistence being the measure of our belief in ourselves, we readily engage and successfully overcome whatever obstacles may appear before us. Becoming a *disciple* of persistently practising *discipline* leads us to achieve what we formerly believed impossible. When we achieve to this extent, a state of calm certainty is experienced which opens up our skills to using the final key.

Decisive Intent

'What is meant by the saying "The one who turns his back on the world hears the whole world run after him"?' asked Second Merchant Lee Mok.

'This can be understood from our perspective,' answered First Merchant Fu Jung, 'by watching two people bargaining. A peddler at Yellow Court market, for instance, comes up to you with an object, and you say how beautiful and intricate it is, that you like it and how much will he take for it. As soon as you have said this, the peddler wants you to give as high a price as he is intent on getting from you.

'Yet, when you turn your back saying that you do not care for it, he comes after you asking if you will take it for half. If you continue turning your back, he will offer it to you for a quarter, or even less. Such is the greedy nature of this world. You follow it, it runs from you; you turn your back on it, it comes after you. Both require intent, but only with decisiveness will you master the latter.'

'So one must have a decisive intent,' said Lee Mok. 'But how can one attain such a quality in a world of constant persuasion?'

'By developing calm steadfastness and certainty of purpose,' replied First Merchant Fu Jung. 'For in truth, having the inability to decide will put you at the mercy of the many who will smell your indecision coming towards them. Even as though you had slipped in the dung-heap of destiny.'

*　　*　　*

Life is a series of choices. The quality of both our personal and our working life is a result of our previous decisions. For it is our decisions, and not our conditions, circumstances, education or background that determine our future. As a species we are unique in our ability to choose to live by the consequence of either our own decisions, or those of others. Most of us, however, forfeit the majority of our lives by choosing the latter, allowing others to decide for us. Many consistently argue that often there is no choice, but as the world will accept no neutral, even *not* choosing is making a decision. It is choosing to be indecisive.

Being decisive is a fundamental skill that is both learned and improved through practice. But instead of developing the skill, many of us unwittingly *decide* to spend our time improving our complaining skills over those decisions taken by others that affect us. Infinitely more time and energy will be expended by a group discussing someone else's decisions, than by making them personally. Indeed, the person who is prone to complain is almost always indecisive.

Without doubt, as a race we can be divided into those who are decisive, and those who are indecisive. Being in command and feeling secure in ourselves is part and parcel of being decisive and having a firm intent. People recognise when you have these qualities and chase after you. But they also clearly recognise when you do not, and are able to keep you where they want, or get from you what they want. The degree to which we are indecisive is in direct proportion to how insecure we feel, whether consciously aware of it or not.

Being unable to decide means having uncertainty in ourselves, indeed being unable to trust in ourselves. Too many of us, though competent to do anything, end up doing nothing because of our inability to decide. Like Dante's starving man, perplexed at which meal to eat first, our own 'Divine Comedy' is alarming, for the majority of people are unable to decide what life they want to lead, even with all the options laid before them. It is little wonder, therefore, that decisive intent is rare. Yet it is by far the most sought-after quality in leadership, and the very ignition that sparks will and sustains constancy. Decisiveness is personal surety.

Developing decisiveness is an essential part of developing will. It is possible to divide will into three parts: volitional will, static will, and dynamic will. Volitional will is that part of will which moves us to action. Without it there can be no act of will. Deciding to return and finish something you have started, or simply returning to work after lunch, are examples of this element.

To measure the strength of our volitional will is to observe whether our bodies respond immediately and positively when we decide to do something, rather than ignoring or contradicting our mind's decision. Very simply it is the will that causes you to get out of bed in the morning when you'd rather not. To want something is not the same as to will it, you may want to speak a language, for example, but if there is no volition to learn it, then you won't.

No volition can be put forth without an expenditure of energy, and this is where static will comes in. This is the part of will that contains the energy for action. It is here that energy is accumulated and stored. The static will cannot be engaged without volition, and neither can a volitional will be enacted without drawing its energy from static will. To measure our static will's strength we should observe the level of mental listlessness, or resistance, when involved in something which does actually interest us.

When volitional and static will have joined together to set a course of action into motion, dynamic will ensures its completion. It is that part of will that does not give up. Its strength can be measured by observing how consistent our efforts are in following our decisions through. All three parts of will form an energy cycle that keeps us moving forward. Static will accumulates energy, providing it to the dynamic will, which expends it in a series of co-ordinated and concerted individual volitions.

The real test of will intent always comes down to the strength of the volitional will, which means the ability to make choices, preferences, discernments and decisions. The degree to which you allow yourself to remain indecisive is in direct proportion to the low reserves of energy in the static will, and infrequent spurts from the dynamic will.

Thus, the less we make decisions, the less we are inclined, and the less energy we have. Even when we make decisions, we will lack the energy to see them through. Subsequently, we lack steadfastness and calmness of purpose, tending to wait for something to happen rather than making it happen. Without decisiveness, the remaining energy of our will is channelled into procrastination, complacency and apathy, causing us to complain and worry.

There are two simple keys to becoming decisive. One is continual practice and the other is to take absolute responsibility for the outcome of your decisions, irrespective of the consequences. Developing decisive intent goes further. It means taking ownership of your intent and being fully accountable for all outcomes, even if what you decide is delegated to another to perform. It does not mean looking for the out before you start, like a prenuptial contract. It means accepting that, even if everything is on the line, you still win because your decision is in harmony with your values, convictions and fundamental beliefs.

Duty to Resolve, Will and Decide

Both will-power and decisiveness are as vital to each other as yin and yang. They are complementary parts essential to their greater whole. *Resolving to will to decide* something, therefore, is the simple key to overcoming indecision and developing an iron-clad will. An indomitable will is that *useful* part of the ego discussed in the seventh scroll. The education and development of will is one of the objects of our existence, for nothing is impossible when a person says *I will*, with all the force, energy and determination of his or her character.

In turn there can be no finer way to build our character, as gaining mastery over each attribute of will develops strength in the others. Thus, willingness builds discipline; discipline builds perseverance; perseverance builds decisiveness; and decisiveness strengthens willingness. Similarly, volitional will builds static will, which in turn drives dynamic will and strengthens even the silent will, that unseen force of intent, truth and goodness that nothing can resist.

It is our power of will which ignores all the odds, regardless of the fact that they seem stacked against you. Our energy of will distinguishes an individual as surely as muscle power distinguishes the strongest stallion. And our power of constancy, the very key to self-governing success, encapsulates all the elements of will, discipline and decisiveness. Ensuring that we develop such power and energy to the full is more than our personal responsibility, it is the very duty that we each owe to ourselves as human beings.

> *The human will, that force unseen,*
> *The offspring of a deathless soul,*
> *Can hew a way to any goal,*

Though walls of granite intervene.
You will be what you will to be,
Let failure find its false content,
In that poor word, environment,
But spirit scorns it and is free.

It masters time, it conquers space,
It cows that boastful trickster, chance,
And bids the tyrant circumstance
Uncrown and fill a servant's place.
There is no chance, no destiny, no fate,
Can circumvent, hinder, or control,
The firm resolve of a determined soul.
Gifts count for nothing, will alone is great,
All things give way before it, soon or late.

What obstacle can stay the mighty force
Of the sea-seeking river in its course,
Or cause the ascending orb of day to wait?
Each well-born soul must win what it deserves,
Let the fools prate of luck. The fortunate
Is one, whose earnest purpose never swerves,
Whose slightest action, or inaction serves
That one great aim. Why, even Death itself
Stands still and waits an hour sometimes
For such a will.

Anon

The Ninth Scroll: Holding the Carp

The Secret of Cultivating Your Superconscious

鯉

'To be out of Trader's City and fishing feels good,' exclaimed Su-Lei. 'It was a good idea of yours. Let us hope the carp are as big here as you say.'

'Of course they are,' said Wing, 'for carp are like ideas. They expand in relation to their limitations. They grow twice as big in a large lake such as this one, as they do when they are contained.'

'But we have some enormous carp that swim in a tank at our House of Trade,' protested Su-Lei.

'Ah, but they are imported from the lakes,' answered his friend, 'like imported ideas to have around us. Their spawn, however, stay small because of their contained environment, like so many conditioned ideas.'

Su-Lei cast his line across the lake as he considered his friend's words. 'Though we are good at getting on with things, it is true we lack some bright ideas. Sometimes we get one but ... look! I have hooked a big one.' Su-Lei excitedly pulled in his line, which was taut as the large fish strained to free itself. Holding it still in his hands a few minutes later to remove the hook, the captive suddenly jumped, slipping out of his hands and back in the water before he could stop it. 'It's gone. I had it and lost it and it was a good one too,' said Su-Lei with frustration.

'Were you still talking about your ideas, or your fish?' said Wing.

'Ah, and just so,' said Su-Lei. 'Ideas can be like a slippery fish. It seems that unless one holds tight, what one has will get away, ready to be caught by another with a firmer hand. Why, only the other day I saw something selling at the market which will bring much fortune to the trader. Yet, at the same time I recognised it as the culmination of an idea that had come to me months before. If only the timing had been better for me and I had not been so busy, it could have been my product.'

'But it did come at the right time,' said Wing, 'as the answer to what we want does every time. Your inner guide, Su-Lei, is there to aid you with everything, including your decision-making. Problems only come when we fight against our inner sage, second-guess it, or never hold on to what it says because we are too busy.'

'That's all very well,' argued Su-Lei, 'but being in business successfully means being busy — a busy man catches more fish, as they say. But how do you recognise this "sage" and its "answer" from all the voices that occupy the mind?'

'By daring to ask it the right questions of course!' replied Wing.

Since ancient times there has been talk of the human mind being part of a more powerful mind, a Universal Mind. Access to this mind is understood to be through our superconscious, the very medium of our soul's awareness of *everything*. Our enthusiasm and excitement, our intuition and insight, our creativity and imagination, and our motivation and inspiration are influenced by this genius, that each of us has the power to draw from.

Genius is considered rare, simply because Man is not consciously aware that he has the capacity for it. Yet everyone without exception has had an idea come to them and done nothing about it, only to see its physical reality months, or years, later. That experience alone reveals that each of us has a connection to a wider world than just our conscious mind. There is an inexhaustible wealth of potential within us, just waiting to be tapped into.

We all have voices in our minds. Often they are the internalised voices of our parents, teachers, and both significant and insignificant others who have influenced us during our formative years. Some of our inner voices are helpful and supportive, others are demanding and critical, often unhelpfully so. Listening to these voices can severely contain us within fixed limits, not allowing us to expand to our full potential.

It is, therefore, important to distinguish between the critic within, which must be silenced, and the guide within, which must be cultivated. This guide can be likened to a sempiternal sage who keeps up to date on current events in the lives of people. Being able to recognise and interpret our sage is one of the most important factors in expanding our boundaries and taking charge of our lives.

It is through the superconscious that our intuitive faculty comes, a faculty that can be deliberately cultivated and consciously trained. Intuition is a capacity each of us is born with, like the capacity for breathing and eating. For most of our lives we are not consciously aware of them. When we do take care to breathe properly, our physiology improves dramatically, indeed lymphatic functions, essential to our health, improve over one thousand percent. When we take care to eat properly, our mental and emotional well-being improves significantly.

Reclaiming conscious control over innate powers increases them. As you read the pages of this book, for example, you are using a number of complex mental functions without being consciously aware that you are doing so. One of these functions, your memory, instantaneously compares each word you read with countless words stored in your memory bank. Associations and images are continuously served up, with the word's meaning, into your conscious mind. Similarly, intuition continuously serves up data to your conscious mind, even though you're completely unaware of this process. The key is to learn how to become conscious of this.

We were given intuition for a reason. Like our other senses, it is first and foremost a survival tool. Our ancestors' daily survival depended on how tuned in they were to their surroundings; the most intuitive survived. Intuitions arise as they are needed and are meant to guide us. As a survival skill, intuition is especially adept at addressing the future. For most of us the process of gathering information not immediately available, takes place unconsciously, and with much interference from our rationalising logic and emotional impulsiveness. The fact is that in being consciously intuitive our ability to make accurate decisions is significantly improved.

It is a misconception that intuition is a power we acquire, as it is already an integral part of our psyche. A further myth is that women are more intuitive than men. This misconception is based on the belief that the former come up with intuitive solutions more consistently. In the same way that men have been taught to show their strengths while women have been taught to hide theirs, men may refer to hunches and gut feelings rather than admit to intuitive insights, until recently associated with feminine realms.

The strange fact is, the less you know about a subject or topic, the more effectively your intuition comes into play. That is why a partner, regardless of sex, can *know* the right course of action when their advice is asked for, because they are removed from it. In being so they are able to heed their intuition as part of their decision-making, rather than be persuaded to ignore it because of the weight of solid evidence.

The skill, however, is to combine our intuitive powers with our powers of reason and feeling to improve decision-making. Mathematical analysis, for example, should only get us to a point where our intuition takes over. Although everyone is intuitive, only a few learn how to access and interpret it effectively. But business today, demands that people are intuitive as well as analytical and rational. Decision-making should involve intellect, emotion *and* intuition: does it add up, does it feel right and does it *sound* right? We live in an age where the limitations of traditional logic and rational guidance are becoming painfully clear. Increasingly, proactive businesses are no longer dismissing our natural modes of guidance as something intangible and unreliable. What was formerly considered as solely a feminine attribute is being rediscovered as a rigorous method fundamental to future survival as well as meaningful and valued growth.

An intuitive is simply someone who *consciously* uses intuition in his or her personal or professional life. All of us use our intuition unconsciously, which is why the promptings that come from our sagely guide are so faintly heard at first. Even though they are clearly audible on their own plane, we tend to disregard them as trivial. This is the tragedy of Man. The voices that so often misguide him into pain and self-limitation are both loud and clamorous. The whisper that guides him to material and spiritual harmony is timid and soft. Cultivating our superconscious allows us to develop our particular intuitive strengths through an unlimited source outside our general experience. Such deliberate cultivation requires the conscious practice of three important keys.

Confidently Trusting

'Forgive me my General,' said Ho-Yen, 'but you look greatly troubled these days. How so? Is this battle not just another skirmish for you?'

'I fear that the state of Kou-Wu will soon be no more, for our rivals have great strength,' answered the General.

'Allow me to suggest, my Lord, that you enquire of the oracle of Zig-Zag Mountain,' said Ho-Yen. 'It is said that his foresight is never wrong. With an answer in hand, you will know how to fight.'

'Surely that sagely legend holds no truth, although I would seek any advice at this time,' sighed the General, 'for I am so uncertain as to what tactics to follow for the best.'

Having travelled to Zig-Zag Mountain, Ho-Yen reminded the General, just before he was about to enter the mystic cave alone, that he could only ask one question of the oracle.

'Indeed, I have only one question,' replied the General, 'and it is the one I have been asking myself for days now as ten thousand troops gather. Will this great battle be won?'

Many months later a very bedraggled Ho-Yen was found on Zig-Zag mountain by one of the oracle's disciples, employed in gathering herbs.

'What has happened for you to lie so forlorn on the track leading to my master's cave?' he asked.

'Your master was wrong,' said Ho-Yen bitterly, 'and I came to tell him so. He answered yes to our great general, yet the battle was lost! Kou-Wu is no more, it belongs to the province of Yuen.'

'Forgive me honourable sir, but in truth my master answered correctly,' said the disciple. 'A great battle was won, even though the victor was your general's rival.'

'But it was I who suggested bringing him to this infernal place,' said Ho-Yen. 'He came here trusting he would receive an answer to his benefit, not his ill.'

'Yet to come here is to not trust yourself, for my master speaks only *what other men already know but lack the confidence to accept,' said the disciple. 'Had your general asked the right questions of himself he would have received the answer on the right course of action. Had he trusted himself he would have asked more specifically. As my master says: Be careful what you ask for in life.'*

'I believe at the end he knew the truth,' said Ho-Yen resignedly. 'As he lay wounded he told me, "Good friend, in truth no agency can be trusted better than your own source, no matter how great it is. I refused to trust my own, so refrained from asking it, in case it told me something I did not want to hear. What use are ten thousand troops when a man leading them cannot follow himself?".'

It is a paradoxical truth that the best leaders are the best followers, and only when we confidently trust our own inner guidance do we become able to lead ourselves. It is difficult to find the right answer, however, after years of schooling have conditioned us to fear questions. Many people fear filling out intrusive forms, now part and parcel of our information demanding society, because of the pressure of putting down what has to be the *right* answer.

As the world is becoming increasingly specialised, it is more difficult to remain an informed participant. We hand over decisions to experts and specialists who *know better*. In doing so it becomes unnecessary for us to rely on our own infallible guidance power, and subsequently we trust it less and less. Many people become unable to make decisions concerning their lives without the opinion of others, whom they in turn blame when things go wrong. What makes the life of one person different from another is largely the questions we ask ourselves. Thus, the important thing in life is knowing what questions we should be asking.

A question effectively phrased can already be half answered. Ambiguous questions can be interpreted in more than one way.

Will I be happy? Should I go into business? Will I get married? Should I move jobs? Will I have enough money? These kind of questions that all of us ask of some 'oracle' at one time or another during our lives, are not specific. But it is not just a matter of good grammatical English and syntax. Questions need to have received investment from feeling, emotion and logic. The famous Delphic Oracle in the very birthplace of logic and rational philosophy, ancient Greece, illustrates the fact that rational thought and intuitive thinking can support each other.

The key is to use the intuitive and the reasoning parts of the mind as a team, rather than one against the other. Both are necessary as yin is to yang, female to male, emotion to logic. Intuition tells us what to do, while reason tells us how to go about doing it, helping us to find, clarify, determine and research. It is important to understand that the two work together, while recognising and accepting each other's peculiar characteristics and different methods of approach. One moves in a non-linear fashion, the other in a rigid sequence pattern.

Hence, all projects should be examined under this duplex light, which is infinitely better than our habit of always asking others what they think. In performing the latter we consistently refuse to build the self-confidence we need to even take our own advice, let alone heed it.

The truth of the matter is that it is an unnatural condition not to know which way to turn when we are faced with different courses of action to pursue. If the fault of this lies within us, then the correction must lie within us also. Put simply, it is a great pity that we do not have second thoughts first. Not trusting our own intuition comes from not believing in ourselves, or believing that we do not really deserve what we would like to happen. In asking 'should I go into business, or should I take the new job', for example, we are immediately saying that we have not thought out what we really want.

It is important to understand why we want to make a move and what we think it will do for us. This raises personal questions such as: does the kind of security and compensation I can expect, fit in with my primary goals — those things that are important to me? Should I take this job if I want to spend more time with my family? Will this move provide me with the experience I am seeking?

Intuition is activated in response to questions and is goal-directed. But as it responds by presenting us with impressions and images, we must be consciously aware of our questions in order to understand the signs it gives us. Otherwise, and this is what usually happens, we send out conflicting signals. For example, 'I want to earn more, but I don't want more responsibility'; 'I want a pay rise, yet I want more time with my family'; 'I want a relationship, yet I like my independence,' are demands that we are not often conscious of expressing.

In traditional Western thinking, answers follow questions. With intuition, questions follow answers. A question will raise impressions which in turn suggest more questions. But it will do so in a non-linear fashion, not in the more rigid sequence associated with reason. So it is important to be absolutely clear about what we are consciously asking and why. In this way, we can understand and interpret the impressions we receive and be prepared to address the new questions that subsequently arise. In leaving one job or relationship for another, an intuitive answer may pose the question that there is something we must funda-mentally change about the way we are going through life.

As there is no stronger soul to direct us than our own, it is important to build the self-confidence to trust ourselves. This can only be done through developing clarity of purpose and understanding the motives behind the goals we want to achieve.

In essence this means working towards being consistently true to ourselves. The degree to which we are is in direct proportion to how tuned in we are to the Universal Mind and its infinite storehouse of knowledge.

When we are busy being somebody for everybody, we can neither be ourselves nor trust ourselves. As we are unable to trust what our inner guide unerringly advises, we allow our preconceived opinions, formed of intellectual pride, prejudices and beliefs, to build a barrier. With this barrier standing in the way of true wisdom we look upon others as masters and sources, instead of the teachers and agencies they really are. Developing a confident trust in ourselves through clarity of questioning and a willingness to interpret our intuition, however absurd it may initially seem, is academic, of course, unless there is adherence to the second key.

Sincerely Listening

'If only you had contacted me earlier,' said Counsellor Tang. 'You would have been welcome to have had the position. Indeed, it would have made my job considerably easier. But please understand that I cannot change what I have now done. The seal has been set and, of course, it would be unfair for the new licensee.'

Merchant Fou-Ha was livid with himself. How could he have been so stupid not to have followed up his strong impression of last month? That licence was just what he wanted, but how could it be that Counsellor Tang was the authority to grant it? Why, it wasn't even his province, which is why he had ignored the inclination to go to him. He had not listened to it, reasoning that if he asked Counsellor Tang, then the whole court would know and he would certainly lose all opportunity of obtaining such a licence.

'Perhaps the new licensee may consider negotiating with you,' suggested

the Counsellor. *'I don't believe he has the experience you have so indeed he may welcome the alliance.'*

Merchant Fou-Ha's anger started to turn towards what he considered was utterly unfair. He began to feel outrage, reasoning that the two had obviously cheated him out of what should have been his. In the instant before letting rip a verbal rendition of what he thought of this bureaucrat's heritage, he sensed another impression. Almost like a voice, it urged him to keep quiet and not say something that he would later regret. But his anger overruled the voice and the cutting words were already out, quickly flying to their mark. With chilling accuracy they hit it. Almost immediately they were regretted.

'Ho Sir!' exclaimed the Counsellor in surprise. *'Such dragon's teeth as those should be removed. To dare to question my authority is one thing, to slur the name of my ancestors is one more. The sum of both will cost you dear!'*

Later Fou-Ha rationalised that his words, although said in the heat of the moment, had been well deserved. Following his outburst he had ignored his feeling to ask for forgiveness, reasoning that it would only show further weakness. His silence had compounded the situation and now he faced a heavy fine.

'It could have been worse you know,' commented his friend, Trader Yen. *'He is clearly a fair counsellor to show such leniency in the loss of so much face. Perhaps he thinks you have lost more.'*

'What does it matter what he thinks?' said Merchant Fou-Ha, *'I am worse off than ever thanks to him. First I don't get the licence for not talking to him, then I get a fine for talking to him. Some counsellor!'*

'With respect,' replied his friend, *'I feel that I am unable to agree with you. Your whole problem has nothing to do with you talking or not talking. It has to do with you hearing, but not sincerely listening.'*

Every one of us, some more frequently than others, experience the feeling or urge to contact someone. It may be someone in authority, for example, and we choose not to act, preferring to let 'sleeping dogs lie'. Often, the very next day, or at least soon after, we receive a letter or phone call from that very same person.

We kick ourselves for not having contacted them first, annoyed at being pre-empted, giving away the advantage. Sometimes we do take the initiative, but delay in contacting someone only to learn that the person had been thinking of us earlier. People in tune with each other will often make contact at about the same time about the same thing. The fact is that all of us hear what to do, but only a few listen.

Preferring to go with what we think we ought to or should do, we delay and thus obscure our feeling. We then invite other mistaken, conflicting beliefs to provide reasons for not following our intuition. So, although everybody hears their intuition, most people spend their time reasoning why they can't do something, instead of intuitively finding out how they can. There is both good sense and reason for the Eastern belief that the less you do, the more you achieve, until you reach the point where in doing nothing, you accomplish everything.

What underlies this is the belief that when you are in tune with the Universal Mind, everything flows in the best way. If you apply this wisdom to the business world, its truth will be revealed. Seasoned successful executives, for example, do less than they did when they were climbing the ladder of success, yet achieve considerably more. As they follow their 'hunches', so they have more time available to think, without the company of others. Being highly productive rarely involves high activity, yet often activity is mistaken for productivity.

The majority of people do not take the time to retreat from the company of others in order to get ideas and inspiration. They are too busy doing what they do to become what they can. People fail to tap into their innate superconscious for inspiration, because they prefer to confer with everybody and everything else but themselves. Many go to great lengths not to be alone, to always be surrounded by others. Yet only by developing our aloneness can we learn to tune into our inspiration power.

Despite the proven fact that one flash of insight can clear up a thousand difficulties, people continue to be active in addressing each difficulty one by one.

Having time alone is not about being lonely. It is a beneficial solitude and is by far the best way to learn how to activate your voice of inner guidance. It is possible, with practice, to hear this voice to the point that you recognise it regardless of surrounding noise. But to begin, there must be solitude. Ask yourself how often you take the time to be completely alone without any artificial influences whatsoever, and just listen to your own thoughts, without going to sleep.

Tens of thousands of travelling business people have the perfect opportunity to do this. Yet on the plane they eat, talk, watch a video or sleep; on a train they read, talk, phone or dine; immediately on entering a hotel room they turn on the television, computer, pick up the phone or return to the company of others as soon as possible.

Recognising that the majority of the best ideas come while 'out of the office', is leading many organisations to send staff on executive 'retreats'. These are great opportunities to talk, share ideas, discuss strategies, plan future objectives, develop shared values, improve processes and systems, plan to increase productivity, reduce in-house politics, bond team members, motivate, inspire and improve communication. But do they? They are highly effective because they put people in a different environment, but they are seldom retreats. Most are simply boardrooms away from the office, where the intention is that participants can remain undisturbed, though in reality this is not the case. Even the rooms at the venue are set up to look the same as the office, because that is what is expected.

Moreover, despite the prior understanding that attention should be on the process of the retreat, most people are unable to comply. The common excuse for this is, 'I'm sorry, but I must stay in contact with the office as they might need me for something important.' So each break is used as an opportunity to phone the office. With faxed and internet messages, countless calls to take and make, and lots of time in the bar to discuss problems back at the office, there is seldom the opportunity to *retreat*.

In our information-driven world, where technology allows us to perform a hundred tasks in the time it used to take to perform one, we still do not have the time to develop those invaluable inspirations that will propel a business way beyond what was previously imagined possible.

This state of affairs encourages people to live at a breakneck pace, with the days and nights crowded with things to be done or things to distract us from doing. Aloneness, not loneliness, is often very difficult to procure, and many would feel unhappy if they had it. Some of us cannot bear silence or being alone for more than a few minutes. Indeed, some organisations unable to play music, play a background 'white' noise in order that there should be no embarrassing silence during meetings.

Outside the traditional office environment, a new syndrome has arisen for the 'teleworker'. A growing number of people working from home are apparently developing 'loneliness' symptoms through lack of interaction with others. But loneliness, regardless of environment, is ultimately a state of mind. Having to redevelop a relationship with one's self through the opportunity to be alone is to be embraced, not feared. Amazingly enough, the deep silence of a quiet place is something many of us have never known. Most will argue that they haven't the time because their responsibilities fill every waking hour. Yet a greater responsibility is to reorganise our lives so that we are able to retreat to a quiet place, and once more learn how to get in touch with our self, simply through listening.

Indeed, by calling a halt, being still and listening, our

loads are lightened. We see how best to complete our work without struggle, effort and with greater enjoyment. The flashes of inspiration that bring us what we want are just that. They are more responsible for propelling the world toward solutions than the constant hustle and bustle involved in trying to find answers through external means.

Arguably, most of the above is plain common sense. But when it comes to developing our innate powers, what is common sense is not common practice. Despite recognising the fact that deep down each of us has an intuitive power that will unerringly guide us, we deliberately choose not to develop it. Instead, we promise ourselves the time to develop it one day in the future, for we are too busy to think about it now.

We have to resolve to build the habit of sincerely listening to ourselves every day. This is important, as all intuitive guidance is like manna in the desert and needs to be acted on as it occurs. The more you embark on your daily retreat, the more you will come to like it. Conversely, the less you go, the more you will come to loathe it. If you are unable to develop the time to go mentally fishing for a set period each day, then it is doubtful that you will catch any worthwhile ideas. As your habit develops, you will discover that you become more accustomed to listening to your intuitive voice.

This is not because your intuition is talking to you more, it is because you are becoming more accustomed to recognising how it speaks to you. It may come in the form of signals, impressions, symbols, objects, reading a book, talking to another person, idly noticing something or a strong urge. The secret is to stop, on the instant, whatever you are doing or saying at that moment, and reorient all your attention to the message. The incomplete act, the broken sentence, should be left, for this is an exercise in evaluating something sincerely.

That is the real secret for developing your connection to

the superconscious — learning how to shift your attention when you feel, notice, or become aware of an intuitive message. You shift your attention by listening with absolute sincerity, the same sincerity you would bring to your marriage vows. For, in truth, they have the same value. The guidance coming through to you is that spiritual part that only wants the very best for you, as one who loves another would want. And, as in the building of all relationships, that involves the third key, risk.

Faithfully Risking

A traveller who had recently entered a foreign province was accosted suddenly by another traveller who told him in a frightened voice, 'We have wasted our time in this direction, for behind those dark clouds is a vast mountain which will block our way.'

The first traveller felt strangely calm, a calmness that he had not fully experienced before. A while ago he would have reacted with great concern, but this time he felt no artificial sense of impending doom. Surprised at the report, though, he thanked the frightened traveller and continued on his journey to see whether it was true or not.

He came upon no mountain, but he did meet another stranger who reported gloomily, 'It is hopeless to continue your journey. Just beyond that meadow is a precipitous canyon that even the nimblest of goats are unable to cross.'

Once more experiencing a sense of inner calm, the traveller decided to see for himself, and went on his way leaving the stranger disapprovingly shaking his head. There was no canyon at all on the path he took, but he did run into a third stranger in a military uniform, who sternly commanded, 'Stop! You are forbidden to go any further in this direction. This path leads straight into the camp of an army that will punish your attempts to continue.'

Not frightened by the threat the traveller walked past the fuming stranger. He met with no camp and there were no soldiers to block his path. Travelling on his way he encountered a fourth traveller. But this person seemed no stranger, indeed the man felt as if he was entering the presence of a long lost friend. As he approached, the other traveller extended his arms in welcome, saying, 'Because you decided to take no-one's word for anything, but to test everything yourself, my wait has been brief.'

'But tell me,' asked the traveller, 'who are you, although I feel sure I know you. Have we met before?'

'Of course,' came the answer. 'I am your faithful guide for life. What you have risked confirmed your faith in me so I am able to become fully present. Come, let us continue, there is no insurmountable obstacle ahead and so much to share with you.'

We will recognise the voice of wisdom when having to make a decision, by the fact that it emanates from deep inner calm. Impulse, on the other hand, is frequently born of undue excitement. The intuitive traveller need not fear nor hesitate when meeting strange things which try to block his or her journey. The key is to simply be aware that they are there, both inside and outside, and walk right past them. Learning to faithfully risk the guidance of our intuition requires us to be like Bunyan's Pilgrim, who met and left behind impeding temptations. Understanding that there is no-one who has any real power over you other than yourself, allows you to pass beyond every fearful obstacle and travel forwards.

Confidence in one's self is built through risk. We must be ready to risk mistakes because we may not always have the right intuition. If we disbelieve our intuition, however, then we will not have it at all. Nothing of any meaningful consequence can be attained without risk. Indeed, the greater risk can often be in not taking a risk, for whatever is necessary for us to do, is also *possible* for us to do. Risk builds faith and in turn faith allows us to risk. When we become accustomed to faithfully risking that which the powerful superconscious affords, we overcome ourselves. In overcoming ourselves, we overcome the world.

There is no single pattern that an intuitively guided life must follow. Sometimes we will see, in a flash of insight, both our course and destination. But at other times we will only see the next step ahead and will have to keep an open mind, both as to the second step and to the final destination. It is at these times that one must believe in one's *self* enough to risk the second step in the faith that, although the answer may not always come when we need it, it will always come when the occasion calls for it.

Whenever we reason or feel that we are taking a risk by following what we intuitively think, we should do so anyway. Even if we are later proved mistaken, it is the only way to practise and develop the level of confidence and faith in ourselves essential for our intuitive capabilities to fully present themselves in the long-term.

The Right Hook For Certainty

There are opposites in all things, and in everything there exists the spirit of the opposite: in man the quality of woman, in woman the spirit of man; in the sun, the form of the moon, in the moon the light of the sun. The closer one approaches reality, the nearer one arrives at unity. The evidence of this is shown when no sooner has a question arisen in your heart, than the answer comes as its echo, within or without. If we look before ourselves, the answer is before us; if we look behind, the answer is behind; if we look up, the answer awaits us in the sky; if we look down, the answer is engraved for us in the earth; if we close our eyes we will find the answer within us. It is only a matter of climbing a mountain, and the name of this mountain is 'why'.

As a child we begin the process of distrusting our intuition, relying on others for our answers. Re-learning to trust confidently in our self and what we are capable of actually doing for ourselves, also demands that we listen to our self both with consistency and sincerity. Those rare times when we have been able to be sincerely honest with our self remind us once more that regardless of the question facing us, the answer lies within us.

We *always* know the answer, but only by learning to have faith in that answer, irrespective of what risk we might perceive in it, will we hear it with clarity. Such is the paradox of any gifted power, that unless we declare our faith in it by heeding its guidance, it will not perform. There is no lock, or even door, to this superconscious energy that willingly delivers abundant creativity, inspiration and guidance. The only requirement is to be aware of and receptive to its flow. By shifting our attention when we feel this flow, we consciously cast our line into its depths. Such certainty will always hook the right answer.

The Tenth Scroll: Taming the Bull

The Secret of Harmonising the Yin and Yang
of Communication

牛

'Toeless Wong was crippled for allowing Duke Ling's prize bull to run amok in the kilns,' said Yen Ho, in answer to his fellow disciples' question. 'Indeed, it is said that he lost a toe for every one of the ten Imperial vases that were smashed.'

'In truth, it was through having his feet stamped on by the mighty bull while he bravely fought to recapture it,' said their Patriarch, upon overhearing their discourse.

'By my ancestors,' exclaimed Yen Ho, 'what courage!'

'Indeed yes,' said Wei Tzu, 'but fighting yang with yang is not the way to communicate and overcome.'

'It is said that yin and yang connect all,' said Yen Ho, 'but please explain how, in the context of such a difficult situation.'

'The mutual seeking of yin and yang depends on opening and closing,' began the Patriarch. 'Opening and closing are the natural principles that influence the rise and fall in all of heaven and earth's ten thousand things, including man and beast. Yin and yang should always be harmonious. For the opposite of one redresses the balances of the other.

'When the bull was in yang mode, so was Wong. Rather than adopting yin mode, he fought charge with charge. He pitted his aggression against the

199

bull's aggression. When yang is hard and aggressive, only the yielding softness of yin can calm it. As a seasoned keeper, Wong knew full well how to calm the bull. But seeing the crashing commotion before him he forgot, and was as a fool rushing in. In doing so, he was no different to the bull.

'Yin and yang modes can be taught to be switched on or off, according to what is needed. Yin or yang must be used as appropriate to tame that part within all of us which can be likened to a charging bull, and to soften the raging bull within others who appear to be attacking us. Men do not mirror themselves in running water, they can only see themselves in still water. Only what is still can calm others to stillness.

'Always remember that it is important to know when to speak and when to remain silent. When you want to hear others' voices, return to silence; when you want to be expansive, be withdrawn; when you want to rise, lower yourself; when you want to take, give; and when you want to overcome, give way.'

All through school we're taught to read, write and speak, but apart from how to listen critically, we are never taught to really communicate. Yet the way in which we communicate inwardly and outwardly directly influences the quality of our relationships with others, as well as with ourselves. True communication, however, goes way beyond our variety of listening skills.

All of us have a dormant bull within us, desperate to be heard and we usually allow another person to turn it loose. Those people who are prone to arguments, will claim that any heated intercourse, be it debate, discussion or family tiff, requires such stimulation. Healthy arguments making for healthy relationships is a myth, however, as when two people allow themselves to become angry towards each other, there are two losers. In the same way that it is pointless to fight fire with fire, being angry with others burns our valuable psychic body into a charred shell.

Understanding the nature of how things interact helps

us to harmonise those universal forces that can strengthen us, instead of allowing an imbalance which hurts us. The very nature of communicating with ourselves through listening to our inner world, for example, reflects directly on our interpersonal communication with others. The principle for listening is the same as evaluation. You cannot evaluate others until you have successfully evaluated yourself; and you cannot listen externally until you have mastered listening internally.

What is not said can be clearly audible in our inner stillness, and what is not said is more valuable to us than whatever is being said. Through inward and outward stillness we become able to listen to others without influencing what they say by our reactions. For example, the speech of others is yang movement, for it is outward; one's own silence is yin stillness, for it is receptive. When the statements of another are inconsistent, if we reflect and enquire introspectively, then an appropriate response will be forthcoming.

To use stillness to listen to what is being voiced means exercising our ability to look at matters from all angles, without entertaining any associations or attachments that may affect our understanding. Yang is opening up, yin is closing down. Opening up involves assessing people's feelings, closing down involves making sure of their sincerity, and not believing that we must get our point in first, particularly during an argument.

Learning to communicate fully instead of having to manipulate partly when we are with others, means being ourselves. Without doubt that is the first and most important step in effective communication. But it also means harmonising yin and yang so that our inner and outer world remain balanced.

Emptying Fullness

'Give us a tale, honourable sir,' said Yen Ho, 'as to how Man can know when to be silent and when to speak.'

'Silence and speaking relate to the emptiness and fullness of Man,' began Wei Tzu. 'If your mind is filled with your own prejudices, the truth that others speak cannot be heard. When engaging in conversation, most people are in a hurry to express their own opinion. As a result they don't hear anything but the sound of their own voices.

'Imagine a man, with his hull full of stores, crossing the Yellow River,' continued the Patriarch, 'and an empty boat happens along and bumps into him. No matter how hot-tempered the man may be, he will not get angry. But, if there should be someone in the other boat, then he will shout out to them to haul this way or veer that. If his first shout is unheeded, he will shout out again, and if that is not heard, he will shout a third time, this time accompanied with a torrent of curses. In the first instance, he wasn't angry; in the second he is. Earlier he faced emptiness, now he faces occupancy. When he is faced with occupancy he allows the dialogue of his fullness to take over: how he considers the state of things should be. If a man could succeed in making himself empty, and in that way wander through the world, then who could do him harm?'

'But Man seems to always want to speak more to blame than to praise, regardless of what he brings on himself,' said Yen Ho.

'Exactly so! Which is why one must learn to speak sparingly,' added Wei Tzu. 'A word is a bird. Once let out, you can't whistle it back. Measure your words. Think that every word is a coin and once it goes out, it won't return. For in certainty speech is priceless if you speak with knowledge. As such it must be weighed in the scales of the heart before it comes from the mouth.'

Through the process of listening to others a large percentage of our hearing is overrun by a constant evaluation of the incoming messages we are receiving. 'What does he think he is doing? Do

I agree with this or that? Why are they saying this or that? Why don't they make their point? What is it that happened to me that is similar? Why doesn't she let me get a word in? That tie doesn't suit them, and so on. Constant internal chatter creates a fullness where an emptiness is required.

Where is the usefulness in a vase for flowers? It is in the empty space that receives them and not the pleasant external façade. As we would feel the mood of an empty house, we can learn to see the emptiness. When a group of people sit in a circle, either around a board table or in any meeting, it is the climate or the spirit in the centre, the empty space, that determines the nature of the group's atmosphere. The fruitfulness of a business meeting, for example, can be clearly determined by the atmosphere during the silences. The difficulty is that meetings, particularly in the West, are not considered to be about silences. Indeed any pauses in some meetings are simply seen as opportunities to either drive points home or as signals that the meeting is terminated.

It is because of the non-ownership of what results from a meeting that further meetings are then often planned. The business world is full of meetings where although the *atmosphere* of it may not be heeded at the time, whatever is perceived from such an atmosphere is soon discussed afterwards in the privacy of quiet corners. In the same way that we refuse to hear our higher self whispering to us in the silent gap between our thoughts, due to our internal dialogue, we miss important elements of what is being related to us by others. Then, whatever we do miss, we tend to compensate with our own interpretation of what we think others said.

As infinitely more is communicated by what is not said than by words alone, it is important to listen to the empty parts or silence. Conditioning in the Western world, however, has taught us to be uncomfortable with silences during an active conversation. Silent communication is something that inscrutable Eastern sages engaged in as a matter of course. They would remain silent *after* the person they were talking to had finished speaking, in order to listen to what they were hearing within as well as without. Although common in psychotherapy, modern Man generally prefers to prepare his reply *before* the person he is speaking to has finished. His internal dialogue is amplified when what is being said strongly opposes the listener's own point of view.

This is because most of us tend to believe that listening means listening *critically*. In searching for what we agree with or, more predominantly, disagree with, we feel we are paying attention. Indeed many people only feel that they are offering worthwhile support when they are pointing out the flaw in an argument. But bearing in mind that they prepare their answer based on their own opinions drawn from their own circumstances and based on their own frame of reference, the proverbial 'baby' of an idea can be often drowned in their full, overflowing 'bath'. There is nothing wrong with pointing out a flaw, except when the whole focus of attention is on doing so.

As our tendency is to listen to others within the boundaries of our own experience, we keep strengthening the root of most communication problems. Because we see the world as we are, not as it is, we find it hard to listen with empathy. Clever listening skills may have taught us to keep quiet while the other person is talking, but most of the time our listening is tuned to something we want to hear, something that is useful to us, or someone we want to impress, sell to or gain something from.

This fairly cynical view is because the majority of us are only interested in improving our communication skills to further our own interests, in other words — 'what's in it for me?' To have empathy means to empty ourselves of any hidden agenda whatsoever. It means moving into the hearts and minds of others to genuinely begin to see the world as they see it, not as we think they should see it. Often, when talking with another we are itching to get our point over as to how to sort out a problem, by relating how we sorted out a similar one.

Our conditioning has further taught us to believe that we must get our point in first, particularly during an argument. The way we see things is all that matters to us. We believe that taking the time to listen to another while not defending, attacking or judging, conveys acquiescence and agreement with their viewpoint. In thinking that listening to others in order to understand their feelings denotes weakness we are communicating predominantly in the full yang mode. To develop the receptive yin mode we need to calm ourselves. In this way we can listen to people, assess the myriad of things that they want to say, measure their abilities and see their intentions clearly without misunderstanding.

It is amazing that one of the world's largest and most lucrative professions, law, has developed because people are unable to resolve their disputes through their own communication. This would certainly seem to be a fact of our conditioned life that is now well and truly entrenched within our culture. Man will generally look to blame, instead of looking for a solution, in the same manner that he will spend more time getting out of something than getting on with it. It is certainly worth asking ourselves how much of our time and energy is wasted in some kind of defensive or protective communication, internal squabbling, interdepartmental backbiting, politics or interpersonal dispute. Then if we take the time to pick any one of those disputes or arguments that come to mind, it is worth asking ourselves if we are capable of resolving the situation without external assistance.

Admittedly, there are those irritating situations when one is dealing with faceless adversaries, such as the computer which may be 'down at the moment'. But generally, if we empty ourselves of our hidden agendas a solution can be reached. The fact is that when we take the time to shut down during a conversation, we know how to resolve it. The aphorism of 'least said soonest mended', however, is often not considered when communicating. Instead we prefer to issue advice, or take issue with what we believe is being said.

Silence is Golden

There was once a loyal servant who worked for a wise counsellor. Each day different people would visit and pay handsomely for the advice they sought. After fifteen years of working hard without asking for wages, apart from what the house provided for him, the servant declared his intent to return to his wife, sons and home village again. Being asked for all the wages that were due to him, the wise counsellor was pleased to give his servant the enormous sum of two hundred gold crowns for his years of good service.

But just as the servant was about to leave, the wise master asked him if, after all these years of showing people into the house who sought counsel, he was going to depart without hearing a word of advice from his master. Not wanting to offend his former master, the man agreed and asked for counsel.

'Ah, good, for I have two pieces of advice for you and you can have them for my usual fee!'

The former servant paled, but feeling cornered by his own decency and his trained instincts, accepted in order to please his employer.

'First,' said the master, 'you are listening now aren't you?'

'Yes I am most certainly listening,' said the servant.

'Excellent! Now give me one hundred crowns for the first exquisite jewel of wisdom. Good, I thank you. Now, always remember, don't meddle in other people's affairs. Leave them to their own lives.'

'Don't meddle in other people's affairs!' exclaimed the servant. 'Why, I

could have heard that from any second-rate fortune-teller for a hundredth of the cost!'

'Ah, but at this price you will be sure to heed it,' came the reply.

'Will I now?' gasped the servant under his breath, then resignedly bowing to his fate, added, 'and the second piece?'

'Always remember,' said the counsellor, while pocketing his faithful servant's last remaining one hundred crowns, 'to save your anger until the following day.'

As the servant shook his head in disbelief, his former master said, 'Now then, I can't let you return home empty-handed. Here is a cake for you to take and share with your family to celebrate your home-coming.'

Taking the heavy cake, without as much as a glance, the servant called upon his years of dedication to thank the old man and set off on his journey. Inside he was both seething and aching. 'Fifteen years for this, fifteen years.'

After a few days' travelling the servant entered a forest. As daylight began to fade he began to feel uneasy. Eventually walking in almost total darkness along the narrowing road, it was with relief that he glimpsed a light ahead. But as he approached the cottage window, from whence he realised the light shone, there was something distinctly unwelcoming about it. Lost, however, he knocked on the door which was opened by an enormous man with a face set in a frightening grimace.

The servant's grim host motioned to him to sit at the table and ladled him out some soup. To the servant's astonishment not a word was spoken. As he was finishing his bowl, a muffled knock from under the floor made him start. As the big man opened a hatch in the floor, he saw to his horror a ragged misshapen creature slowly emerge. In the faint shadow of the room's solitary candle he recognised it to be the shape of a blind, mistreated woman. The servant watched, dumbstruck, as the big man reached up to the shelf for a human skull. Ladling soup into it he made the woman drink it through the eye before pushing her back into her subterranean prison.

'What my friend, do you think of that!' said his host.

'I'll tell you what I think,' said the servant, about to give the man a tongue-lashing for his cruelty. But just as suddenly he found himself remembering the words of his former master: 'Don't meddle in the affairs of others', and said, 'I think that you must know what you are doing. You must have a very good reason for it.'

'I do indeed,' said his fierce host. 'And you are the first guest in a long while to survive my hospitality. That creature you glimpsed was my wife. Years ago I caught her with her lover ... that is his skull she uses as her soup bowl. What do you think of that!'

'I think that you did the best thing you knew how to do,' answered the servant.

'You are a very sensible man. All who have disagreed with me have been buried out back with their throats cut. Now, let me show you to your room.'

Having departed early the next morning, the servant continued until he at last began to recognise familiar landmarks. The dull ache of fear left him as excitement at being with his family grew within him. Despite hurrying, it was late when he spotted with joy the welcoming light from his home. Through the window he immediately recognised his wife and was overcome with emotion. Then, through his tears, he suddenly realised that there was some sort of party going on, and to his horror he saw a younger man walk towards his wife and embrace her. Everyone in the room applauded as they kissed, laughed and began to dance round the room to the music.

The servant was beside himself with anger. 'All right, I have been away for many years, but with another man, right in front of my eyes! I'll kill him! I'll kill her!' Pulling his knife out and pointing toward the heart of the man dancing with his wife he prepared to rush at them. At that very moment he heard his old master's words: 'Save your anger until the following day!' Forcing himself to hold his hand and resheath the dagger in his belt, he said to himself, 'All right, I will save my anger until the following day, but only until then!' He then ran back into the woods to spend a restless night, determined to satisfy his honour the following day.

Not falling asleep until dawn, he awoke mid-morning and began to walk briskly through the village. As he did so he came across an old neighbour friend who recognised him.

'After all these years I don't believe it!' said the neighbour as he embraced his friend. 'And what a time to return just as your son had graduated from the House of Scholars. His mother was so happy, she danced half the night with him.'

'By the gods!' said the servant, shocked that in the heat of the moment he had almost killed his own son and wife. 'My master's words were indeed worth everything I had,' he thought to himself.

Rushing up to his home there was a moment of profound silence as the door opened, followed by shouts of welcome and joy. As his family shouted for more celebrations, the servant remembered the gift from his former master. 'I have the perfect thing!' he said, and lifted the heavy cake out of his bag. Grasping his dagger, the servant cut through it and pulled out the first slice. As he did so gold coins began to roll out all over the place. When the astonishment had subsided they counted the gold, which came to two hundred crowns exactly.

The true worth of advice can never be fully appreciated unless it is well paid for. Indeed, the propensity to ignore good advice is in direct proportion to the frequency with which it is freely given. When advice comes free it is never valued and seldom heeded. In giving all his wages for his master's advice, the servant naturally felt he had been cheated. But because it had cost him so dear, he remembered and heeded it.

There is a far deeper meaning, however, with regard to his application of the first piece of advice. The intuitive, feminine or yin part of us, so vital in making our own decisions, is very often repressed, abused and imprisoned underground, a tortured representation of our locked up feelings. We instead ask for the free advice and opinions of others, who are as free with their advice as to what we should do, as we are with our advice to them.

When we suggest something that is not what people want to hear, they can, metaphorically speaking, go for our throat, killing off our worth, and burying us in the back of their minds as one of the reasons they have their problem. The best form of advice is in itself a valuable listening method and is applied by all leaders and achievers, who realise that as we have two ears and one mouth it is best to use them in that order. It is simply: 'What do *you* think you ought to do?' That way people come up with their own solution, leave satisfied, and thank you.

The importance of keeping our own counsel and trusting our own intuition during our interpersonal communications is paramount to harmonising yin and yang. Without them we are at constant risk of jumping to conclusions in all areas of our lives. Before asking advice of others, ask yourself if you are prepared to pay for it. Upon receiving it, ask yourself if you truly value the worth that you were prepared to pay for it. Then observe if, when the occasion arises, you ignore or heed the advice.

Become aware of listening to your own advice, to see if you really have the courage of your own convictions. Observe also if you are a person who prejudges situations without fully investigating the fact. Observe also if you have a tendency to suggest to others what they ought to do. Then, if you become aware that you have this tendency, notice how you are actually the one that suffers most of all. Next time you have the urge or compulsion to raise questions, or argue a point someone is making, practise holding your tongue and instead listen to what is really being said. You will discover a commnication that is far more satisfactory than the outer discussions and arguments of people who know not what they discuss.

When you are able to practise these elements in your daily interactions with others, you will be well on the way to understanding the natural flow of communication. To learn the skills of effective communication means following the 'sowing before reaping' principle — listening before speaking. Where the mouth is the mechanism, the ears and the eyes are the assistants of the heart and mind. When these three respond in harmony, they act in a beneficial way. To listen primarily with the eyes and heart and secondarily with ears, means listening on four levels: physical, emotional, mental and spiritual. When used in harmony, all levels allow us to hear what is really being said, rather than merely hearing superficially.

When we first hear something, we hear it on the physical level. We hear the actual words, the softness or loudness created by the vibration of speaking. Then we hear the feeling, belief and enthusiasm at the emotional level. At the mental level we notice what is important to us. Much of our schooling ensured that we hear well at this level. At the spiritual level what we hear wakes us up to what we already know; we may not fully understand what is being said, but something tells us that it makes sense.

Whenever we are playing a role and not being ourselves, it is not possible to hear on all four levels because our attention is diverted. It is diverted to ensure that our role is not discovered by the person we are communicating with. We are not usually aware of this as it is an automatic response, but it has a dramatic effect on our ability to listen. Ask yourself, 'Do people communicate by what they say, or by how they really feel about what they say?'

Never Explain, Never Complain

In a small temple lost in the mountains, four pupil monks were practising Zazen. They agreed amongst themselves to observe seven days of silence. The first day of meditation began auspiciously but, as night began to fall, one of the monks began to feel annoyed that the lamps were not being lit.

'It was your turn to light the lamps,' he complained to one of his colleagues.

The second monk was surprised to hear the first one talk. 'In my concentration on not speaking I forgot,' he explained.

'Listen to you two,' said the third pupil. 'Why did you talk?'

'I am the only one who has not talked,' concluded the fourth.

Most of us find it hard to remain silent, even when we have promised ourselves to watch what we say. The degree to which we are externally influenced, rather than internally motivated, is in direct proportion to our need to complain about things or explain ourselves to others. Consider how much of your daily communication, for example, is taken up with explaining yourself. The cause is partly our deep-rooted blame culture and partly because we are concerned about how we appear to others.

Human beings prefer to live by echoes rather than by silence, as when hearing none, they feel insecure. A man may invent an idea of himself as being pleasant, dynamic or popular, or unapproachable, stern or difficult. He then broadcasts his idea of himself to the surrounding world. While preferring an agreeable echo from others, he will also accept a critical one, for anything is better than hearing nothing. When we learn to live without needing the echoes of others to confirm our belief in ourselves, we no longer experience fearful dependency on others.

The fact is that whatever anyone thinks of us, it is none

of our business. This is a strong statement, and should not be misconstrued as an edict to be irresponsible towards others or ourselves. In all principles the Golden Rule stands firm. But we cannot know what goes on in the depth of someone else's mind, or heart, from moment to moment as well as they do. Nor can they know exactly how we feel from moment to moment. Infinite combinations of conditioned experiences create unique frames of reference for each of us, even though there is universal connectedness. It is therefore impossible to try and keep everyone happy all of the time. Only by becoming entirely unconcerned about what others *choose* to think of us from *their* frame of reference, are we on the path to becoming our own person.

It is worth remembering that at any one time we are either in control of ourselves, or being controlled by another. There is no neutral. A person can quite easily give up control, for example, by inventing the self-image of being a desirable person, which others can then control through flattery. But what can others control if a person is comfortable just being themselves? The fact is that we communicate more about ourselves in the moment before we speak, than in the ten moments that follow. We cannot fail to communicate clearly to another, even without words, particularly when that person is attuned to what is *really* being communicated. This is because meanings are not found in words, they are found in people.

What is communicated in the moment before we speak? Either trust, confidence, sincerity and compassion; *or* distrust, nervousness, insincerity or thoughtlessness. When there is high trust and confidence we can almost communicate without words. When trust is low, communication is exhausting and ineffective. Trust and confidence need to be communicated first, because people don't care how much you know until they know how much you care.

With improved communication high on the agenda of businesses anxious to reduce manipulation, departmental rivalry, contest and positioning, political backbiting and destructive gossip, many staff members understandably attend courses. These initiatives, which focus on listening skills and team-building, are well intentioned, but their effects are often short-lived because they seldom pay attention to the lack of self-trust people feel. Self-trust is the basis of trust towards others, which is in turn the basis of effective communication.

When we learn to know and understand ourselves, we begin to trust ourselves. When we begin to have confidence in our own feelings and act on them, we are becoming self-reliant. When we are self-reliant and enjoy this self-trust, we no longer worry what others say about us because we are increasingly our own person. Such a pathway naturally leads to less negative complaining. Whenever we are not satisfied with how we genuinely believe things should be, any form of constructive complaining can be applied in a positive light. But the majority of our daily complaints do not relate to this. We allow our powers of communication to be occupied by trivia, obsessed by how things *should* be.

Most of the time we complain out of habit, a habit that weakens us, literally draining us of our positive energy. Yet we are all conscious of doing it. Like the four pupil monks, we unwittingly compromise our good intentions by the need to complain about what others should, or should not be doing, and the need to explain to others why we did or did not do something. With our entrenched habit of 'putting people straight' and constant invitations to 'explain yourself', it is difficult to spend just one day with good intentions, let alone a week. But taking one day to consciously not explain or complain will show how significantly different we can feel.

Without doubt, our quality of life is determined by the

quality of our relationships. They provide us with our greatest joy and our deepest sorrow. The less we complain and explain, the more sincere we become. When we become sincere with others, openness and trust builds and communication is developed with or without words.

Balanced Worth

We cannot communicate more than we are, so it follows that we must seek to understand ourselves in order to recognise who others are. This requires learning to listen to our self, rather than the roles we adopt in order to please everybody. We need to understand that communication is infinitely more than simply words; it is the ability to transmit ourselves successfully to others and receive their feelings and thoughts clearly. For how we truly express ourselves is the manifestation of how we each individually think and feel. This means acknowledging that we communicate much more by our silence than by our speech. In doing so we begin to harmonise the yin and yang of communication, instead of allowing our yang, outward movement, of speech to dominate, thus causing us to miss so much of what is really being communicated.

In feeling the need to offer advice as freely as we may previously have done, we have to accept that communication must be unconditional. To truly listen to another requires us to empty ourselves of the assumptions, prejudices and opinions that each of us carries around, waiting for the opportunity to use them. This in turn involves knowing our own position, by questioning our beliefs in order to understand how they may distort our communication with others.

In this way we can learn to appreciate where others are

coming from. For without doubt, the secret to good communication is making the person you are talking to feel valued, without compromising your own worth. To do so successfully is to balance the yin and yang of communication. For only when both are working in harmony is it possible to tame the bull within you, and calm the bull within others.

The Eleventh Scroll: Freeing the Bear

The Secret of Reaping Strong Relationships

熊

Kung was alarmed to hear the husky growl that awoke him. Even with the shortcut he had taken to C'hu, it was an arduous five-day journey, so that when he found a tranquil spot in which to camp, he had fallen asleep almost immediately.

'By the gods!' he exclaimed, 'what devil is that?' as the angry roar continued. Adrenaline soothed his immediate panic as he braved himself to investigate further. It seemed that the roar was not approaching, rather it was changing to a crying roar. His search led him to a clearing where he saw an enormous bear caught in a vicious bamboo trap. Fearing for his life, his immediate thought was to flee, but upon hearing the bear whimper, he stopped in his tracks. Summoning up all of his courage, he began to speak consolingly to the bear and noticed that the bear's big brown eyes were full of pleading.

What he did next, however, would make him wonder for many years what had ever possessed him to do so. Perhaps it was because the creature seemed to sense his genuine compassion, that it allowed Kung to get close enough to remove the trap. Immediately he had, the speed of the bear took his breath away. In an instant the bear held him in a life threatening hug. Expecting his body to be crushed at any moment and torn limb from limb, Kung momentarily realised how mad he had been. Then, just as quickly, the animal released him, sniffed him, limped across the clearing and disappeared into the heavy foliage. Kung, however, saw the bear's eyes in his dreams for many weeks, for it had been thanking him, not hurting him.

Ten years later, Kung was visiting C'hu, where his cousins had a surprise for him. 'From your old story, cousin, we know how you like to fight bears!' they teased. 'Come, we are going to see Keeper Lok who is visiting with his bear show.'

Kung was appalled at the state of the mistreated creatures which had obviously been whipped into submission. During the show, one of the larger bears suddenly raised itself to its full height and sniffed the air, as if recognising something. As it did so, Keeper Lok viciously pulled on the chain running through its nose ring, causing it to roar with pain. Perhaps because the beast could no longer take such injustice to itself, it drew on its final spirit and with an enormous growl from its now toothless mouth, tore itself free. With blood spurting from its ripped nose it rushed at its cruel keeper, squeezing the life out of him in seconds.

While the mesmerised crowd panicked, Kung stood absolutely still. The eyes that had already searched him out were not pleading to him this time, they were thanking him. Having recognised Kung's scent, the bear had gained the courage to free itself this time. Within moments the great bear had lumbered away seeking its escape.

Kung knew in his mind that the bear's freedom would be short-lived, that it would be hunted, caught and destroyed. But in his heart he knew that the unconditional service he had performed for the bear had atoned for the seemingly malicious ways of Mankind in the eyes of the bear. The bear had never forgotten him and had taken strength from his kind act of long ago. Since that day Kung himself had made a habit of providing unconditional service towards others, despite their growling. Since that day he had never been afraid, nor considered it a weakness, to show kindness or serve another. It had taught him, above anything else, that with all relationships there was risk. But it was a risk worth taking. In the last ten years he had met with peasants, dukes and marquises. He had even conversed with the Emperor. But all of them he had looked upon the same in his heart, knowing that every person *was a living creature that had the right to be treated equally, regardless of their station.*

Most of us are unable to free ourselves from our hidden agendas of insecurities, anxieties, desires and hopes, particularly in the work arena. Because of this we are more reserved, shy, suspicious and cynical towards others we meet for the first time, than we are relaxed, confident and open. Apart from the hugs we dutifully give relatives in appreciation of their annual gifts, we are basically backward in coming forward in respect of our affections towards others.

We reserve our warmth and affection for those who are very close to us, reserve being the operative word, for even then we never consider being *too* demonstrative. After all, it isn't the done thing. How is it possible, therefore, to focus on being customer-oriented and develop strategies to build long-term relationships, when we often can't be spontaneous even with those we love?

The fact is that our lives are given true value by what we do for others and our relationships with them, not by our relationships with our possessions, our accomplishments and our careers. These are only valuable when they serve as a vehicle to enhance our relationship with ourselves and other people. Increasingly, in our heavily biased commercial society, we have placed things and accomplishments above people.

By understanding that absolutely no-one is in our life by accident, we can begin to accept that human relationships are part of why we live, as only through them can we grow and awaken. Some people offer us greater lessons than others, giving us the opportunity to become more tolerant, accepting, understanding and, ultimately, loving.

Given that our primary purpose here involves the teaching and learning of love, it is clear that we can only achieve that purpose with the help of others. Regardless of how much Man, through his self-sufficiency, considers himself to be an island, he can only be fully developed and realise his full potential through help, support, belief and love. But how much do we truly value others?

The more we value something, the more we devote our time and attention to it. We must ask ourselves, therefore, what message we are sending to our children, spouse, family and friends, when we spend fifty to seventy hours a week in our work-place, and only a few hours with them. Of course we love them, but the clear signal is that we fear failing more in business, than we do in our family.

In the work arena people are increasingly aware of the truism that customers don't buy companies or products, they buy people. However, the clear signal sent to the customer is continually at odds with this. In the same way that people will be more interested to see their own image on holiday photos, family or conference videos, customers are more interested in getting what they want, rather than in helping a company to grow. Yet they are still treated as a means to an end and they know it. Most companies do not know how to be customer-focused, or build long-term relationships, because the majority of people do not know how to serve. The only way to serve is to *want* to serve. But how many can really do this, when the belief that serving others is tantamount to being servile is so entrenched?

People will not generally help others unless there is something in it for them. Indeed it is so rare, that when it happens it can become headline news. In showing interest to buy from a commission-only salesperson, he or she begins to warm to us. When that interest does not spark, there is coolness towards us. When we receive good service from others it really does make our day and we tell the world about it because it is so rare and unexpected.

Without question, the ability to provide unconditional service towards others is the key requirement for success in business and in life. This means knowing how, and wanting, to develop strong relationships regardless of outcome. It is important, therefore, to define service, unconditional service and a strong relationship. In going to collect our car after its service, we find it finished. The points we drew the service department's attention towards have been dealt with as expected, and the cost is just what we anticipated. The man behind the counter is busy, but makes time for us and is reasonably polite, again as expected. This is good, but this is *not* service.

Service is doing the unexpected. When we return to find that the car has been fully valeted, with a letter or gift on the seat thanking us for our custom; or when the assistant takes the time to treat us like the most important person in the world by being genuinely pleased to have served us, and asks if there is anything else they can do for us, including collecting or delivering our car for us next time, we feel 'Wow! This is great', as a chore has been turned into something pleasant. With such an attitude we have no doubts about returning. We don't feel that we are budget fodder or a statistic, we feel worthy. That's service!

The difficulty is that what one customer service department considers good service is nowhere near the quality of another. But the fact is that under emerging customer demands, they will not survive. In reality, good service costs less, firstly because the biggest value comes from the individual's enthusiasm, and secondly because people do not mind paying extra for the pleasure of receiving good service.

This is what was intended by giving a tip a tradition originating in the eighteenth century at country inns, when the carriage driver or horseman would toss a coin to the stable boy. This advance payment for service was to ensure that everything would be cleaned and ready for the following day, with the horse fed and watered. The incentive encouraged performance and the word 'tip' became colloquial slang for the practice: To Insure Performance. In more recent times the tip has become a *right to receive* which people pay out of customary politeness more than anything else. Indeed the tip is now added to the bill as a service charge in many establishments, irrespective of the quality of service.

Unconditional service means to do what you do regardless of whether you receive a tip, payment, praise or recognition. Perhaps because of its heritage, our culture is predominantly inclined towards the need to be right and superior, rather than towards providing good service, which is considered subservient. That is why the customer is reticent about complaining, because it requires confrontation with the person serving who, inherently resenting criticism, feels the need to put things right according to the way they see things. The person considered difficult is the person who complains, after all what do they expect?

A further impediment is the demand by many businesses for their customers to provide feedback. Although intended for future analysis, the compilation of results often takes precedent over providing immediate action in respect of a customer's concern. An individual can seldom resolve a difficulty because they have not been empowered to do so. The machinery of procedure has to take over in order to apportion blame accordingly.

Developing long-term relationships is not about scoring points or doing favours for others in order to get them on side. It is not about building a bond based on regular custom. It is about wanting to build success by helping others to become successful. It is about helping people help themselves so that they are able to stand on their own two feet and help others in the same way because of our example. It is about using integrity and understanding, rather than relying on legal documents and contracts To Insure Performance.

Such a shift in thinking about how we deal with others requires certain sowing actions on our own behalf. For how can we expect to reap strong relationships with others unless we first correct the way we grow them?

Daily Service

There was once a man whom everyone in the village disliked because, although rich, he was miserly.

'You must be very jealous of me to dislike me so much,' he told them. 'But when I die, I won't take anything with me. I will leave everything to charity, to be used for the sake of others. Then all of you will be happy.'

But the people did not believe him and mocked him. 'What's the matter with you all?' said the rich man. 'I'm not one of the immortals you know. I will die and then all my wealth will go to charities. Why don't you believe me and wait a few years?'

Resenting the fact that no-one would take him at his word he went for a walk. After a short time a downpour of rain started and the rich man had to take shelter quickly under a big tree. At the other side of this tree was a pig and a cow who were in conversation.

'Why is it that everybody appreciates you all the time, and not me?' asked the pig of the cow. 'When I die I provide them with lots of things — bacon, ham and sausage. People even use my bristles, ears and hide. Yet you only provide them with milk.'

'Ah, but you see, I give my milk daily,' answered the cow. 'Everyone can see that I am generous with what I have, whereas you do not give anything to anyone while you're alive. You give only after you are dead. People don't believe in the future, they believe in the present. Those who say they'll give in the future are never appreciated. And until they realise why they are not, they continue to feel

resentment. It's quite simple, if you give while you're alive, people will appreciate you.'

'By the beard of my ancestors,' said the rich man to himself, and from that moment he changed.

Self-reliance is an attribute coveted since ancient times. Being an individual and standing strong is a favoured theme in our culture, and we achieve this state because others helped us to become self-reliant through the lessons and blessing their lives bestowed on us. Whatever we have of any true worth, we have because others have served us and we have served them. Being a parent is a worthwhile enterprise, even if it appears thankless.

However scarce the daily support, thoughtfulness, discipline and teaching we received from others throughout our lives, they have indeed helped to build the sum total of our experience to date. And it is our experience that remains unique to us. Whenever we hold back that which we have gained through the flowing interaction with others we are effectively hoarding.

The root meaning of affluence is 'to flow to'. Conversely, hoarding means to keep contained. Money is a form of energy, a currency that needs to flow and, like blood, it must flow or it begins to cause serious damage. It flows most effectively when the life energy we exchange for it is in the form of service to others. Every relationship is one of give and take, but it is the intention behind it that is important. Whether it is money, the most recognised measure of service, or compassion, love and friendship, the rewards depend on how unconditionally it is given. Whenever something is given conditionally, the person receiving it subconsciously registers this and the strength of a relationship is affected accordingly.

Because the movement of everything in our external world is done for some consideration or other, it is important for us to choose who we want to do things for, what we want to do things for, and why we want to do the things we do. If we do not address these issues then the growth of resentment within us is inevitable.

That is why most people, when faced by a resentful person, either get resentful themselves or try to lower the other person's resentment through appeasement. Both responses are wrong and are certainly not conducive to reaping strong relationships. The key is to discover why we allow the resentment of another to affect us, and why we may feel resentment for another. For in doing so, we can be free of it.

The rich man was operating under the misguided belief that in promising others something in the future, he could receive their friendship now. But this is the 'someday I will' syndrome, which is strong in word but always non-existent in deed. Building relationships requires current and consistent actions. Writing a letter to someone because we want to, making a call or visit because we want to, giving, selling or serving because we want to, is the only nurturing that is worthwhile.

Whatever we do comes back to us. If it does not come back from one side, it will come back from another. Suppose, for example, we hurt the feelings of someone junior to ourselves by speaking rudely. Because we consider them subordinate, we think we are quite safe and no harm will come of it. But subconsciously our mind is affected by the insult impressed upon it. We carry that impression with us to whomever we meet, where it brings out the same insulting tendency of the person with whom we come into contact. The element attracts the same element, our coldness attracts their unkindness. We may indeed meet and deal with people who cannot insult us because their situation makes it impossible, but when we meet someone who can do so, the experience will be different.

The manner in which we treat the person behind the desk should be no different to the manner in which we treat the person in front of the desk. The view that we are all important customers and valuable suppliers to each other, must be the norm if we are to adopt the emerging values of respect for people and customer care. Allowing them to be simply statements of intent, produced by change initiatives to support erstwhile missions, is surely the height of insensitive arrogance.

Whatever fortunes we are capable of making will most assuredly come from chasing our passion, not our pension. To be motivated to give better performance and service than we are ever paid for will ensure that our commitment and dedication will always be sought after. Knowing that our missions and goals can only be fulfilled through our uncompromising service to others means that we can pursue what we are passionate about, rather than the money.

Many young people commence their career by trying to get the highest paying job possible, regardless of the industry, opportunity, service or product they have to provide. But when we chase money and success in this way we will always be its slave, waiting for the next deal. Alternatively, by doing only that which we feel passionate about, which we love doing and where we are prepared to deliver more than we promise, then the money will chase us because we will always be in demand. The four fingers of commitment, passion, co-operation and dedication are inevitably clasped together into a fist of success by the thumb of service.

Mistaken Identities

Merchant Wang was proud of his adopted son, Tu To. Indeed, he was proud of all of his five other children by birth, but Tu To had done so well. Since being found wandering on the streets of Han Tan, when he could hardly talk, he had become so helpful and supportive.

'You could do better to learn from Tu To's example,' he lectured his

children. 'Consider how he learns the trade so vigorously, the trade I might add that feeds and clothes us all.'

His second son raised his eyes and looked at his father, saying, 'Forgive me sir, but perhaps it is because you treat him more like a customer, and us more like employees.'

Merchant Wang's breath was taken away as the truth of his son's words hit him with such unexpected force. After some moments, he looked at all of his children before him and then addressed his second son, 'Thank you for that, my son, for it is true that a man never believes that he has occupied a certain low level of understanding until a profound truth helps him to rise above it and see the difference for himself. I admit my mistake. I have wrongly been more your employer than your father and have chosen to lecture, instead of listen. From this moment I will try very hard to be a father. But I will need your guidance as old habits stick to an old dog like the fleas it becomes accustomed to.'

'You are both a good man and father already,' replied his son. 'For your actions have always taught us that a man who is good does not go around contriving to be good. It takes compassion to support less fortunate children as your own; it takes courage to admit mistakes; it takes wisdom to want to improve; and it takes love to change for our sake. Together we are all stronger, for a family is greater than the sum of the parts.'

As individuals, each of us are prone to misunderstandings, assumptions, hearing half a story and perceiving falsely what we see. All are seemingly the key factors which cause rifts, disputes and breakdowns in communication. Often, wanting the best for those around us, we lecture more than we listen, certain that the solution we are providing from our own experience is the best. To make mistakes, however, is healthy, for the person who never makes mistakes can never achieve anything worthwhile. In reality, it is not the mistakes we make that are responsible for tense human relations, it is our lack of courage in admitting them.

The mistakes that we make in the misguided belief that

we will get ahead are by far the hardest to admit. The mistake of stealing credit from others will always rebound; the mistake of slandering others through thoughtless gossip destroys friendships, marriages and careers; the mistake of rumour-spreading is as hard to unspread as butter off bread; and the mistake of too much pride has toppled individuals and empires more frequently than any other mistake since the dawn of civilisation.

All of us have experienced regret at things that we have said, not just in the heat of the moment. Feeling hurt we have allowed our tongue to cause damage, failing to realise at the time that the greatest damage is done to ourselves.

Misunderstandings, misconceptions and confusion come directly from our compulsion to react to others. The degree to which we react relates to the degree that we make ourselves see and hear what we believe we want to see and hear. When we allow ourselves to react to another, we are mistakenly identifying that person as a threat, to what we believe are our deep-rooted values, even though we may not be consciously aware of what those values are. Ask another, when they least expect it, what they stand for, and the majority will be unable to answer directly. Asking ourselves is difficult enough. Yet it is our protection of these 'beliefs and values' that causes us to react. The key is to build the habit of standing aside from ourselves, while watching our reactions. By not resisting, condemning, or seeking to change our reaction, we can quietly watch it and let it go. In this way, we do not build internal barriers to listening to another and, through listening, there is less chance of of mistaking someone's identity.

It is worth asking ourselves if our tendency is to treat our own family as family, or whether we prefer to lecture, or listen, to the people we work with. It is certainly worth asking whether our tendency is to react to others because they are family, or because they are not family. Do we react because they are employees, employers, customers, clients, competitors, friends or strangers, or because they are not? Often we give our family and work colleagues less leeway because we know them, while adopting a more convivial attitude towards people we don't know, because they prove interesting, are well-known, or carry a title.

Nothing can be more demotivating than the parent, or employer, who instead of being proud of their child's or employee's performance, dilutes it. Dilution can occur simply from not listening properly, or looking for external reasons for the accomplishment, such as, 'Of course you were lucky to have found that opportunity', 'But you had help from them of course', 'Wasn't it Mr Smith's idea?' and 'Well you must get it from me.'

All these well-meaning admonitions are designed to keep the child or employee in their place, so that they do not get big-headed. The fact is that these sort of put-down admonitions are not well-meaning, as they only succeed in putting the individual down. Such seeds only reap future low self-esteem at best, or even worse, resentment, antagonism and duplication of beliefs.

A helping hand, or kind word sown, can never be overestimated for what it can reap. Merchant Wang's action in adopting Tu To is similar to another story. A poor Scottish crofter upon hearing plaintive cries for help from a young boy, rescued him from a bog just in time. The boy's father, a nobleman, offered to educate the crofter's own son in appreciation. In time, the Scotsman's son graduated from St Mary's Hospital Medical School in London. He later became Sir Alexander Fleming, noted for his discovery of penicillin.

Years later, the nobleman's own son was stricken with pneumonia and would have died, were it not for the use of penicillin. The nobleman was Lord Randolph Churchill, and his son was Winston Churchill, one of the twentieth century's greatest leaders.

None of us can ever begin to imagine how holding out a helping hand towards another can either directly, or indirectly, affect the destiny of Mankind. Conversely, we can never imagine what we are taking away from Mankind because of a thoughtless word, or in refusing to help, even by giving praise. It is worth remembering that every bad habit will lead us away from what we want, and from what we are capable of helping others achieve.

Too many of us spend more time criticising ourselves and others than we do praising, and more time remembering what others did wrong instead of what they did right. We must consistently look for the good in others, refusing to react to just that which we consider bad. No-one has the right to mar another person's life, yet many who have spent their lives doing good are remembered for the one human indiscretion that others insisted must mar it. None of us has the right to cast stones, yet all of us have the occasional habit of picking them up. It is the very act of picking them up that is more the cause of the breakdown in our relations with others than the actual throwing.

In wanting others to accept our foibles and forgive our errors, we must accept the foibles of others and forgive their humanness. In doing so, we are able to let go of our prejudices and compulsions to react, and instead respond courageously by doing, or saying, what is needed to strengthen a relationship rather than weaken it. And how must we respond when we are uncertain what to give? It can simply be a kind thought extended to another in silence, for the energy of such a thought is infinitely more strengthening to both parties than the debilitating resentful thought that is too often sent out.

Choosing and Sustaining Relations

'During one particularly difficult winter a certain man thought about how he could reduce his expenses,' began the storyteller to the listening crowd. 'And he came up with what he thought was a bright idea. He decided to give his hard-working mule a little less grain and hay. This he did and the mule seemed quite content. So, a few days later, he gave it a little less and it still appeared to be happy.

'This continued until the man was giving the animal less than half its normal ration. The mule moved more slowly and was quieter, but the man still thought it was healthy and happy. Then, one morning, much to his surprise, he entered his barn and discovered that his mule had died in the night. This man then wept and cried aloud saying, "My trusty mule is dead, and just when he was getting used to not eating."'

The crowd that now surrounded the storyteller roared with laughter. 'What did the fool expect?' shouted someone.

'Exactly so!' said the storyteller. 'To expect the continued support of such a loyal companion, without any sustenance, is foolish. Yet that is how Man himself often behaves towards loyal friends, measuring the strength of their relationships through the lack of complaint they receive.'

'But Man is not an ass,' shouted another bystander, accentuating the word ass to another roar of laughter from the crowd. 'He does not have to suffer in silence. When he is hungry everybody knows about it. He is like a bear with a sore head!'

'But when he is hungry for something that really matters to him, he is as silent as the night,' said the storyteller. 'People go to bed at night starving for affection, praise and love, more than they ever do for food. For it is their relationships that upset their stomachs more than lack of food.

'In truth, we must never compromise the important relationships in our lives by reducing the level of sustenance every relationship must have to be strong. We must never take the silence of another as agreement of how well we think we are treating them. Indeed, we must never take any of *our relationships for granted, for we might discover that one day the very spark of what was once good has slowly died.'*

True friendship is rare, and a person is considered very fortunate if, during his or her life, there are just a few people he or she can call true friends. But why is such friendship rare? And why do such sayings as 'familiarity breeds contempt' exist? It is important from the outset of any relationship to understand that it must be mutually chosen. It has been said that a person may not be able to choose their family, but they can choose their friends.

If we take the view that the physical plane is a school for souls, then it follows that the spirit will purposely choose a physical host. Doing so helps it to grow and fulfil its ultimate aim of attaining the highest level of consciousness. In this way it will regain the source from whence it came, in a stronger, more evolved form. Its focus is on what will develop it further, as the spirit does not accept that one body is better or worse than another. As such it chooses the most appropriate environment in which to learn and grow.

Our spirit will choose the parents whose make-up, environment, culture and beliefs will be the best influence for growth. The level of friction or harmony which exists, is our spirit's perfect incubator, providing the lessons it needs to experience for growth. Taking the premise that we are each here to teach and learn love, we receive our greatest lessons from our family environment, or lack of it. Taking this postulation to its conclusion means that we do, indeed, choose our family. Furthermore, this belief explains why everyone who enters our life, however coincidental, is not by accident. All relationships serve us with a lesson, or perhaps more appropriately, a blessing in disguise.

However, no one disputes that we can choose our relationships. Difficulties arise when we either do not choose, or do not sustain them with sufficient thought. People will always come together according to the influence of the law of attraction. This law attracts like and, paradoxically, attracts opposites. But the opposites that attract must have complementary energies to sustain them.

This is because this law is, in turn, ruled by the law of harmony. As in music, it is clear when two notes are in harmony. When they are in disharmony, it is also clear. Two notes may not be in harmony, yet when you add a third it makes a chord. In this way, two people may not harmonise, but a third will create harmony between them. Children, for example, can be the harmonious factor between two people, as can be seen by the many divorces that result when the child leaves home. Similarly, two people may be in harmony together, while a third may create disharmony, resulting in a broken relationship.

To discover whether we can be in tune with another requires us to know what we ourselves are in tune with. This means fully understanding our own likes and dislikes. When we are in tune with our own likes and dislikes, we can more easily develop harmony in our relationships. It is because we do not fully understand the meaning of love that it is important to *like* those people whom we believe we love. In essence this means to give to and receive from each other.

Familiarity breeds contempt because a relationship is not balanced, with an equal proportion of giving and receiving between two parties. This is because, although the true nature of Man is to give, the predominant conditioned nature of Man is to take. Thus, one person will interpret the friendliness of another in a different manner to that which is intended, and, often unconsciously, take advantage.

Those couples and partners who are able to stay together are those who have come to respect, and accept, each other because there is giving and receiving in harmonious proportions. That is the basis of all successful marriages, relationships, partnerships and alliances. There must be mutual recognition of what the other needs and brings. Each party sustains the others. When one doesn't, there can follow open discussion and mutual understanding. When this is lacking, then one is inevitably taking the other for granted and the other is allowing them to do so. Both are at fault because they have allowed the discord to take the place of mutual harmony.

How can we be sure that we are choosing a relationship that is right for us? The answer is amazingly simple and relies on three factors. First, each of us has a built-in antenna to recognise that which is harmonious to us. Unfortunately, this remains almost totally ignored. Secondly, each of us feels a particular chemistry when interacting with others. Here, though, it is important to *interpret* the reactions and responses that we feel *correctly*. And, thirdly, we must consistently work at every relationship. This involves effort but not struggle. When you have to struggle to find a solution in a relationship, then the relationship will eventually fail. Even when it doesn't fail there is always pain, which unfortunately we can become all too accustomed to living with.

What is vital to all relationships is that there should be complementary energies. A person who thrives on conflict may seek out those qualities in another that will fuel them. But this will not be complementary. Similarly, a person who seeks more tranquillity will seek out those qualities in another that are conducive to sustaining this state. But conflict-needing and tranquil personalities will not balance each other out either, as they are not mutually compatible energies.

In our concern to ensure that we are in the right relationship, have the right partnership or alliance, we will always tend to seek external advice. Rather than be fully aware of what we are in tune with, listen to our own antennae, recognise the right chemistry and then consistently apply effort, we look to a host of other avenues outside of ourselves. These countless external avenues should only be used to confirm our own internal guidance. To decide whether a relationship is right for us because Mercury is retrograde, for example, makes a mockery of our own capabilities.

Strategic Alliances

Basing a strategic alliance on external advice, when inside you feel differently, is also a mockery. An effective strategic alliance means that you can gain strength, without getting bigger. In the established global marketplace, no single company can go it alone and be successful. What is important, therefore, is to select the best relationships and alliances for each purpose. This involves knowing what makes each party tick, what drives them and what their ultimate goals are. For unless each party is prepared to assist towards the fulfilment of the other's mission, the alliance will not be sustainable. The best alliances are built when the parties are able to provide complementary strengths because of their respective experiences and markets. They involve mutual trust, respect and enjoyment, and must share common values.

A real alliance compromises the fundamental independence of each party and herein lies a difficulty. Management has come to mean total control, and as alliances mean sharing control, managers don't like them. Any alliance is only as strong as its weakest link, and it is individual personalities that make up the relationship links, not legal documents. Unless the people working together understand, like and trust each other, then one will inevitably expect more than the other. Consequently, blame is quickly apportioned when things do not go as planned, with either party being less tolerant than if their own subsidiary were operating in the other's market.

As business alliances are merely a relationship between two energies, the individuals involved must overcome the misconception that control increases success. This need for control is deeply rooted. The very tradition of Western capitalism lies behind it, a tradition that has taught managers the incorrect arithmetic that equates fifty-one percent with one hundred percent control, and forty-nine percent with zero control. With everyone wanting the magical fifty-one percent because it ensures majority control over position, personnel, brand decisions and investment choices, how is it possible to develop the essential ingredients of trust, respect and reciprocity?

Good partnerships, like good marriages, cannot work on the basis of control and ownership. It takes effort, commitment and shared motivation and enthusiasm from both sides if either are to realise the planned benefits. You cannot own a successful partner, any more than you can own a husband or a wife.

Without question, strategic alliances are necessary for business growth, regardless of whether they involve one-person businesses or conglomerates. But the collaboration must be treated as a personal commitment, because it is people that make partnerships work. Mutual benefit is also vital, which means that both parties will have to recognise from the outset that they will have to give something up.

Because markets change and geographic and corporate cultures are different, it is, of course, important to tie up a legal document. Making sure everything is clearly understood and agreed means that unpleasant and contentious issues can be easily resolved. After that, however, something is wrong with the relationship if the legal document has to be referred to.

The fundamental principles of choosing an alliance must be the same as for all relationships — mutual trust and respect.

Whenever we feel that we cannot trust the people we are negotiating with, then despite the rewards that are promised, we must forget the alliance.

The Master of Life

The quality of our lives is reflected in the quality of our relationships. They provide the fundamental environment for our growth, experiences and character, and it is therefore important to choose to reap strong relationships. The degree of pain and heartache we feel is in direct proportion to how weak they are. When those that are important to us are strong, we feel secure; when they are not, we feel insecure. Every relationship we embark upon requires risk, but the greatest risk is trying to be the person we feel we ought to be, instead of who we are. When we feel the need to play certain roles for others, we are not in tune with what we really want. It is more important to please others through being ourselves, than simply for the sake of feeling we have to please.

Taking the risks required involves wanting to help or serve others unconditionally. Relationships that are based solely on receiving something in return are empty. The best way to serve God is to serve ourselves, by seeking to fulfil our purpose of learning love through teaching it. The only way to do this, and truly serve ourselves, is to serve others. Therefore, whenever we have the opportunity to help others to help themselves, we should willingly do so.

This does not mean being available to those people who interpret such actions so as to take advantage of us. But it does mean developing the philosophy of chasing our passion before our pension. It means courageously admitting when we have made a mistake, having the wisdom to improve, and doing so for the sake of our love for others. It means choosing our relationships carefully by being in tune with what is right for us as well as for them. And it means sustaining our relationships by providing the support, affection and thoughtfulness that involvement with others requires.

Ultimately, reaping strong relationships with others does not mean putting ourselves last, or others first, as the occasion demands. It means sowing and nurturing what feels right. It means recognising, understanding and accepting that serving another unconditionally does not make us a servant. It makes us a master of life.

The Twelfth Scroll: Kissing the Scorpion

The Secret of Following Your True Nature

嫐

'You must ask yourself why you behave as you do in order to stop wasting your natural forces,' said Wei Tzu to Merchant Wong.

'But I do get nervous over forthcoming events. How should I act when attending them?' continued to ask the pupil.

'There was once a scorpion,' began the Patriarch in answer, 'who in desiring to cross the river, asked a duck to ferry him over on her back. The duck replied that if she were to do such a foolish thing, the scorpion would undoubtedly kill her with a lethal sting.

'That's nonsense, the scorpion argued, for if I did, what would save me from drowning? You have my most solemn word and sincere promise that I will not repay your kindness with such an act.

'Allowing herself to be persuaded by the scorpion's entreaties, the duck permitted the scorpion to climb on her back. But they were only half way across the river when she felt the cruel sting of the scorpion's tail. Immediately paralysed with just a few seconds to live, the duck asked why it was that, despite his word and causing his own imminent death, the scorpion had stung her. Just before the scorpion itself fell into the rushing waters, he answered the duck, saying that he had had no choice. He was following a scorpion's true nature.'

'So am I to act like the scorpion?' exclaimed the merchant. 'But that means being ruthless, which is not in my nature.'

'It is not a matter of being ruthless or compassionate,' said Wei Tzu. 'It is a matter of acting as you are. The duck was persuaded to follow a false nature. Its true nature was clearly not to let its arch enemy on to its vulnerable back, but it allowed its false nature to dominate.

'In the mineral kingdom, diamonds are diamonds and gold is gold whereever they are placed,' continued the Patriarch, 'yet for each there exists a false copy that serves to confuse seekers. For the true nature of each is disguised and seldom recognised in rough form unless the seeker is both knowledgeable and looking.

'Yet the true form of all precious substances is more recognisable because it has undergone a process to become finer and finer until the refined spirit of the rock radiates its beauty. For all matter is dense spirit, and spirit is finer matter. In the animal kingdom a dog is a dog and behaves as such because it's obliged to be what it is, whatever the outcome. It is indifferent to whether it is rising or falling in the scale of things, to whether it is multiplying or becoming extinct.

'All mineral, vegetable and animal matter obey the law of their species, bowing their heads under the yoke which the wisdom of God imposes. For them there is no evil or sin as in our meanings of the words. There is no need for psychological effort, for their species is fixed. Man, however, can be, on occasion, as frightened as a mouse, as loyal as a dog, as brave as a lion, or as lethal as a scorpion. Man is the sliding note in the scale. This note is precarious, it is a state of responsibility, an octave in which Man can go up the scale or down. As Man occupies so many parts of a sliding scale, human nature is a mixture of good and evil, compassion and thoughtlessness, assist and sting. When his effort is to be himself, he can slide up the scale; when his effort is not, he can just as easily slide down and degenerate.

'We can never know how to act correctly as long as we live with a mind filled with false ideas about ourselves. Following our true nature requires us to overcome the wall that our false thinking has constructed to bar our way. The wall must be scaled with personal effort, for that is the test of our sincerity.'

'But after the wall is scaled,' asked the merchant, 'how is the right path to take known?'

'Because there is a growing sense of familiarity and closeness about everything when we are following our true path,' said Wei Tzu. *'For as we gradually come closer to what is our real home, we recognise it.'*

It is far easier to feel comfortable when we are at home, because we know where everything is. Both our essential and our changing needs are supplied far more conveniently than when we are away. Similarly, we will feel uncomfortable when absent from our *psychic* home, because our true needs are not met. When our true needs are not supplied we seek to fill the void with alternatives. Based on our false beliefs as to what we think will fulfil us, they instead leave us feeling as though something is missing. That is why so many people have a feeling of emptiness in their lives, where instead there should be a fullness.

The way we presently behave is the only way we can, because our behaviour is determined by our psychic level. We cannot act above that level, for we are that level. But it is possible to raise our level, indeed it is our *nature* to do so. In understanding that all things behave according to their nature we can learn to see things as they should be. It requires clearing our minds of whatever has no right to be there, in order to have a clear path home. But it is here we hit a fundamental difficulty, for it is often the weight of our responsibilities that blocks our way.

Paradoxically, the more we become conscious of our responsibilities, the less we are able to recognise the power of wisdom which is already available to us. We can become so busy meeting what we consider our responsibilities, that we have little time to pursue our true path, by far our most important responsibility. Subsequently, we are forced into the ruts of conventional thinking, getting by, and being average.

The question we might well ask ourselves later in life is: 'Why did we spend so much of our time doing things which proved of little value, yet seemed so important?' And the question each of us will surely have to answer soon after is: 'Why were you not simply yourself?' Suddenly excuses such as: 'Because there was never enough time', will become meaningless. We must not learn too late the pointlessness of stating reasons why we didn't become what we were intended to become, or why we expressed ourselves through what we allowed others to impress upon us, rather than from our true nature.

When we do things in a new way, we live differently. We bring no benefits to ourselves until we see something about ourselves that we have not seen before. A person can be told countless times to change their ways, but nothing will happen until they tell themself the very same thing. Unfortunately this usually happens when the pain they are experiencing causes them to exchange their mistaken path for their true one. It seems to have to take suffering and adversity before many people are led to express their true nature, but it doesn't have to. It is important to believe that there is another way to do things, our own particular way. Developing our own path requires us to have the courage and tenacity to live according to three keys – spontaneous non-conformity, volitional responsibility, and vocational balance.

Spontaneous Non-Conformity

An ailing Emperor grew worse despite the efforts of all the court physicians. The court fool suggested that his master might try a physician-sage who had healing powers. Hearing this the other doctors laughed. 'It takes a fool to know one!' they advised. 'We do not recognise this sage as a physician at all,' they added derogatorily. In his desperation, however, the Emperor was prepared to try anything and summoned the sage, who refused to attend him. Infuriated, the Emperor sent a platoon of guards to seize the impudent physician-sage and bring him to the palace.

'I have brought you here because I am suffering from a strange

paralysis,' said the Emperor. 'If you cure me, I will reward you. If not, I will kill you.'

The physician-sage replied, 'In order to treat you, I need complete privacy.' So the Emperor sent everybody out of the room, although the haughty court physicians tried to insist that they be allowed to observe. The sage waited as, eyeing his uncourtly apparel disdainfully, they were led out of the room. When the door was shut the sage took out a knife and slowly beginning to advance towards the Emperor said, 'Now I shall take my revenge for you threatening me!'

Terrified, the invalid jumped up and ran around the room, forgetting his paralysis in his need to escape from the seemingly crazed physician.

Hearing his cries the guards rushed in, followed by all the physicians, advisors and the court fool. 'He tried to murder me!' exclaimed the Emperor, not actually realising that he had been cured by the only method that could have been effective.

The guards were busy ordering, the advisors looking disapprovingly at the sage, and the physicians were busy consoling, while all were trying to robe him. The Emperor continued to stamp up and down in outrage and fear.

'How wonderful to see you up and about again!' shouted the fool above the mêlée. 'You're cured!'

Whoever chooses to be themself must be a non-conformist. The successful leader, the executive, the innovator, is always the exceptional person. That person is not a conformist, except in his or her adherence to their own ideals and beliefs. Society expects, however, that we conform to a particular way of thinking, that we do not act through inner spontaneity but through external consideration. And at what cost do we surrender our individual character by imitating and thus being conditioned by society, which acts in the name of knowing what is best for the individual? Each time we conform to the opinion of others we blur the impressions of our own character.

No-one achieves the lasting rewards of success by being

a conformist. Yet, in business, many people adhere rigidly to patterns they believe some nebulous majority has decreed are prerequisites for approval and success. In this they fall prey to a fundamental fallacy – the belief that the majority is automatically and invariably right. The majority is by no means omniscient just because it is the majority, however. In truth, the line dividing majority and mass hysteria is virtually invisible. If the majority of people in business think one particular thing it hardly guarantees the validity of opinion. More innovative success has been spawned outside of what is considered the 'done' process, by people who remain uninfluenced by opinion, than by following the done process.

The conformist is not born, he or she is made. Indeed, the incessant pressures that bombard individuals, in order that they can be permitted to climb the ladder of acceptance towards success, come from all sides, only differing slightly from generation to generation: 'Yes, you can rebel, but the time will come when you will have to make your own way, and that way must be the established way.' In wanting to achieve success and wealth, young individuals already brainwashed on how they should ensure their security, will adopt the clothes and manner of what is considered to be the successful stereotype. The truth is that we go where we hope to go, and further, when we give up trying to look and act like everyone else.

Being a non-conformist and acting from a natural spon-taneity will get us where we want to go. Spontaneity should not be confused with impulsiveness. The former is a voluntary action without external incitement, the latter is the tendency to act suddenly without reflection, because of external influence. The individual who can think and act independently allows their originality, imagination, resourcefulness and self-reliance to develop.

The truly successful person maintains their individuality,

even though their behaviour may be frowned upon by others. All the shoulds and should nots of conformity repress the individual's feelings of what is right for them as an individual. Each person has their own worth and cause, and must not be timid and apologetic for following their own path.

So often we dismiss our own brilliant ideas and thoughts simply because they are our own, and instead favour the expression of society. And from where does society gain its expression? From a past non-conformist individual who is no longer alive to threaten the status quo. All great individuals who follow their hearts are initially misunderstood, even maligned, before being applauded and leaving their mark. They are guided by what is right for them, not what is right for society.

The leaders and achievers of the innovative and information-hungry business world will more than ever continue to be non-conformist. But to be unconventional simply for the sake of non-conformity is not what it is about. Those who dress and eat differently to others because it is the fashion to do so, or simply to be noticed, are only conforming to the rebelliousness accepted by society. The true non-conformist dresses and behaves, either unconventionally or conventionally because that is how they feel comfortable. That is the way they are. It is not to get noticed, be different or be labelled rebellious. It is just them. Being a non-conformist is having the courage to say 'no' to something because it conflicts with his or her own path, even if the majority would give their eye teeth to say 'yes' to the same thing.

The executive who crosses swords with his or her superiors, may sometimes risk his or her, job in the process. But a business that will fire someone merely because they have the courage of their convictions is not the place a really good executive would want to work. Any organisation where people are afraid to say what they believe, make mistakes, or be radically innovative in the interests of the company, will only be successful in developing seasoned conformists; a place where, simply because a status quo has been established, it must rigidly be preserved.

A good gauge of whether we are being true to our nature in this respect is to become aware of how we behave with others. Getting jaw ache through displaying a forced smile in company when we do not feel at ease, or in answer to conversation that does not interest us, is conforming. The unspontaneous muscles which become uncomfortable to us are a physical manifestation of the discomfort we experience through being what we feel we should be. The inner sensation we experience dissipates our inner energy, which is strong only when we are being our own person.

It is through our spontaneity that we can guide ourselves back to following our true nature, as it is a measure of how much we are internally driven as opposed to externally influenced. Anything is right if it is a correct expression of spontaneity. Unfortunately, many people have lost their natural spontaneity as a result of living amid the contention and rivalry of our conformist-driven society.

The degree to which we are externally influenced is in direct proportion to our conformism. To worry and fret about things that are superficial and trivial, even down to wearing what are considered to be the right clothes and living in the appropriate dwelling, is to cocoon ourselves in the culture of what others consider is best for us. To unquestionably copy those who follow the artificial path that we have been persuaded to think is the only one, is to abandon both our natural path and our individuality. When we relinquish our individuality and the identity of our own volition, we are effectively relinquishing our claim to to being human.

People who follow their own path, relying on their own intuition above the tuition of others, inevitably stand out from the crowd. He or she finds all the doors, which they were told would be closed, opening. Society in turn solicitously, and apologetically, celebrates the individual because he or she kept to their path, choosing to ignore the disdainful and disapproving comments from the wayside. Often it seems to take a 'fool' to shout the benefits of an individual's action, as the 'wise' are more interested in what the Emperor is wearing.

Volitional Responsibility

'But you don't even like the work you have to do!' exclaimed Kan Dou to his cousin, Wong. 'And in truth you have been absent these past three years. You have always told me that you are not interested, so why do you insist on running your father's business now that Manager Ti-Lu is ill?'

'It's very simple Kan! As I am the elder, the role of responsibility falls to me,' argued Wong. 'Anyway, it is his wish.'

Trademaster Yen, overhearing the heated exchange between his old friend's nephew and son, later asked his friend, 'By my ancestors those two fight when the eldest returns. With Ti-Lu so ill, is it wise to have them working together?'

'My friend,' replied the old man, 'you know that it has been my dream that my number one son, Wong, enters the business. With Ti-Lu away this is a golden opportunity. Anyway, nephew Kan's understanding of the business is excellent. Having worked at the House of Dou since a child he knows it better than me or Ti-Lu. If there is any problem, he will be able to guide his elder cousin.'

'Forgive me, but the question as to why you do not simply allow Kan responsibility, arises in me,' said Trademaster Yen.

'Because I can already depend on Kan,' came the answer. 'But I am hoping that in holding a position of such responsibility and power, my first born will be persuaded to return to the Dou Trading House.'

'Let us hope that he respects the order of such factors,' said Trademaster Yen. 'For without the temperance of the former, the latter runs out of control.

The burden of duty comes before its rewards. I trust all turns out well for you old friend.'

Returning from a three-month trip to Chao Province, Trademaster Yen was not surprised to learn of the near demise of the old House of Dou. More interested in the respectability of his position than his duties, his old friend's eldest son had indulged himself using the security of the House of Dou's bonds. The anticipated order from a long-standing client had been cancelled because the irresponsible Wong, ignoring Kan, had caused the client to lose face.

'But it is not my fault,' argued Wong, glancing at Kan begrudgingly. 'If Kan had ratified the order, there would have been no losing of face!'

'To make an mistake is one thing, but to blame your cousin is another,' said his father. 'You knew it was your responsibility to deal with Heads of House, because you are the appointed Head of House! There would have been loss of face if you had not gone. But how could you commit our bonds?'

'What else could you expect?' said Wong. 'You are to blame Father, not I, for how could you expect me to gain the respect of everyone since my return without the trappings of my position?'

Perhaps the most important 'R' we should be taught before those of reading, writing and arithmetic, is the understanding of responsibility. Through our formative years we are taught the ability to react, rather than the ability to respond, so our tendency is to follow the philosophy of: 'It's not a matter of win or lose, it's where we place the blame.' This in turn leads to our willingness to fight for the credit when good things happen, and our unwillingness to accept responsibility for our actions when bad things happen.

This unnatural culture is misguidedly based on the desire to seek early gratification, to minimise risk and to ensure security by making others responsible for the quality of our lives. Paradoxically, we seek to increase our success, while wanting those who we have voted to govern to provide us with more financial security; we demand less interference in our social habits, while pleading for more protection from crime; and we fight for more authority over decisions that affect us, while accepting less responsibility for the outcome. The simple fact is, however, that life's greatest risk is to depend on others for our security.

Only by taking full responsibility for what our life is and is not, in *every* way, are we capable of developing our inherent powers. Only then do we feel secure and develop our ability to respond to risk effectively, regardless of what happens. Whenever we blame others for our life situations, we shift our power to those who we believe are responsible for creating the circumstances.

Being fully responsible means viewing everything that happens to us from the position that there are absolutely no accidents in our lives, and that everything that occurs has a lesson attached to it that we bring upon ourselves. This means accepting that, however absurd something is, our own thought energies have created it. When we are able to do this, we allow our sense of responsibility to grow. In turn it becomes impossible to blame another for either minor scrapes and abrasions or major disappointments in our personal and professional lives.

This is admittedly hard to get understood, for it means that we bring upon ourselves everything uncomfortable that happens to us. With entrenched and firmly established frames of reference, both mental and emotional, ensuring we are not at fault when something happens to us, it is furthermore hard to change. The plethora of work undertaken by the legal and insurance professions stands testimony to this. Yet metaphysically we always relinquish our personal power when we seek to attribute blame or evade responsibility.

For this reason, it is infinitely better to ensure that whatever we get involved with or do, is from our own volition. How responsible we choose to be towards what we do tends to be relative to how much we love, are effective and excel in what we do.

Whether we do things of our own volition or not, we must always take responsibility for our actions. But this is far easier when we do what we are doing because we want to. Developing volitional responsibility means reinventing ourselves to become permanently self-employed team players. This means that we are each our own chairman of the board and managing director, with a lifetime contract to operate our own service company with a single employee.

To hold such a position requires us to set an example in our own lives. It means being proactive, instead of reactive; it involves investing both time and energy in our own personal research and development centre; establishing our own strategic planning division; setting up a human resource department to make sure that our top employee receives continuous training initiatives; starting our own pension provisions; and, of course, providing both customer relations and quality control centres.

Being responsible for our future requires determining a vision and communicating it to our main employee; ascertaining our viability in our industry and thinking strategically. To embrace such responsibility of our own volition, means it is not possible to apportion blame, because such action is instantly recognised as pointless. Indeed, each time the need to either blame or take credit arises, we must ask ourselves if what we are doing is what we really want to do. For whenever our work sparks such insecurity, it is a sign that our response, or Kan-dou-ability, is reverting back to Wong-ability.

Volitional responsibility allows ready acknowledgement that even though there are things in life beyond our control, we naturally have control over our responses. We have, for example, control over our attitude, our tongue, our promises, our energy, our imagination and our choices. What we choose to do with our free time is within our control. Who we choose to have relationships with, to mentor us, to influence us and to either judge, mock or unkindly criticise us, is also within our control. We can control our concerns, worries and actions in the knowledge that it is not any single event that has control over us, rather it is our estimation of the event that we allow to affect us. And this estimate relates to how much our natural ability to cope is in control, or how much our unnatural reluctance prevails. This in turn leads to a state of balance in our lives.

Vocational Balance

'This will be ideal for my meditations,' thought a wandering sage, seeking a cave in the wilderness. Upon entering it, however, he noticed the skeletal remains of many human corpses. Unconcerned, he sat down on a rock to rest from his travels.

'How you answer will seal your fate!' boomed a voice, and turning the sage saw that before him was a gigantic scorpion, the size of a large man.

'As your questions have undoubtedly sealed yours,' replied the sage calmly.

'What manner of Man are you to be without trace of fear?' demanded the scorpion. 'For the nature of Man is to be afraid.'

'Not so,' answered the sage. 'For in truth the nature of Man is to be in balance, and such a state comes when he has no fear of what life may confront him with, because he is in love with the true meaning of life. As my thoughts and actions have led me to this place, how can I fear it? For to do so is to fear myself, which I do not, for I have only love for the person that I am.'

'Then you are rare indeed,' said the scorpion, 'for the men who have come *before you have been escaping from themselves, as one seeks to leave another within a loveless relationship.'*

'You speak as one who has experienced such,' said the sage intuitively, 'for your visage is not strong enough to hide the pain, frustration and indeed anger that you exude.'

'It would seem that truthful perception is yours to command,' answered the fearsome creature. 'Because in truth I was as a man once, long ago, until my ruthlessness attracted a demon seeking a disciple. My resistance to it resulted in having my current condition cast upon me. But because what was left of my original nature was able to resist, the demon was compelled to allow my situation a reversal. Though little use it has been. For of all those who have approached my lair these past long years, none have caused the spell to be reversed.'

'Because no doubt they must answer of their own accord and without direction,' said the sage. 'An accord distorted by their fear.'

'Exactly so! And now you will forgive me if I become impatient to address the riddle I must ask of you!' said the scorpion. 'If you refuse to answer, cannot or your answer is wrong, then I thank you in advance for our debate, for afterwards it will be too late.'

'Proceed as you wish,' the sage said, 'for it is of little consequence.'

'Take heed though,' advised the scorpion, 'that immediately after I have incanted my words I will be rendered helpless in order to allow you to make your choice. Although you are weaponless, there are many swords around you that are sharp enough to enable even the weakest of arms to slice off my deadly tail. And so:

'When you embrace the most deadly, you overcome your worst fears; when you act the least likely, there can be nothing but tears;

When you act from the heart and engage worthy might, then to the end from the start, you have held to what's right;

Your balance to death will be as it is for your life, to do one over the other, can bring sorrow and strife;

When you act as you do because you are as you be, you will know if a kiss or a strike is the key.

'Quickly!' added the now motionless scorpion, looking menacingly into the eyes of the sage. 'You have the opportunity to strike me.'

'My answer is as my action,' said the sage, and calmly outstretched his arms and kissed the creature on its evil-looking head. Immediately the scorpion was transformed and it was now a man that stood before him. With the spell broken, tears flowed freely down the large man's cheeks and he fell at the feet of the sage in gratitude. As the sage helped him up, the large man said, 'You chose correctly, yet why were you so sure, when the nature of a scorpion is to strike when face to face with its adversary?'

'Because deep down you were still a man,' said the sage, 'and it is the nature of a man to love, not strike. And as the riddle implied, transforming you back into a man is the greatest risk to overcome, because Man can be more deadly than any scorpion. Acting in the least likely way of not seemingly protecting myself could only release your tears. Those tears a man has prior to his transformation and the tears of happiness that follow it. Furthermore, because I am in a state of balance I can but only act in a right manner.'

'I am indeed fortunate to have found such a natural individual to release me from my predicament,' said the man.

'Fortune has nothing to do with it,' replied the sage with finality. 'It was your own need to return to your true vocation that attracted you to me, and it was my own thoughts to test my own vocation that led me to you. All of us are interdependent of others whether we are aware of it or not. As such, all of us are both teachers and students, appearing as appropriate to one another when each is ready. That is how we can fulfil our true vocation. Learning how to express it effectively requires a state of balance. For only in such a state can we act as our true nature intended.'

Instead of being frightened by life's conditions it is important to address them calmly, to meet our conditions with understanding, self-forgiveness and love, rather than resignation. Each of us has the power to be master of our life by following our own particular nature. The truth is that nothing is Man's nature except that which he makes for himself. As the whole of nature is made by God, so the nature of each individual is made by himself. Of all the world's creatures, Man is the most entitled to be optimistic about himself, for he is the ultimate representation of God on earth. But he allows himself the artificial nature of pessimism.

Optimism represents a spontaneous flow of love, trust and hopeful attitude. Pessimism comes from disappointment, from a bad impression formed from some hindrance of the past. Perhaps pessimism may show conscientiousness and experience, but can we be in balance if our tendency is to think only of what difficulties may lie ahead of us? The psychological effect of optimism is such that it helps us towards success — surely it was by the optimistic spirit that God created the world — whereas pessimism is born out of the heart of Man.

For the optimistic individual it does not matter if things do not turn out just right, they will take their chance, for life is an opportunity and as such should be seized, not withdrawn from. There are many people, however, who prolong their condition, either of illness or poverty, by nurturing it with pessimistic thoughts. They can unwittingly do so until the condition becomes so real that absence of it seems unnatural. They believe that the state that they experience is their nature, that their misery is their share in life, that they are born to be wretched and cannot be anything else but unhappy.

An optimist will naturally help another who is drowning in fear or disappointment. A pessimist, conversely, upon meeting such a person will sink them even further into their despair.

So on the one side is the kiss of life, on the other the sting of death. The former is natural, the latter is referred to as being realistic. But the only reality is that the very Spirit of God comes to Man's rescue in the form of an optimistic spirit. It does not matter how difficult a situation in life we face, all can be surmounted. What does matter is that we balance the scales of our heart with greater optimism, as the weight of a pessimistic spirit is so much heavier.

It is when we are tired enough, or when the pain of our situation is intense enough, that we will always seek change. The change we must seek to revitalise ourselves requires rebalancing the scales of what each of us finds natural to do, against that which we have the responsibility to do. The measurement for finding and achieving a natural balance through what we do, is how optimistic we feel when we are expressing what we do. We must ask ourselves on a regular basis how enthusiastic we feel about our work, the very expression of our vocation. If the answer is that we are not, then we must take that as a clear signal that our lives are out of vocational balance.

Optimism and enthusiasm go hand in hand because they both emanate from a spiritual source; one feeds the other. It is not possible to be enthusiastically pessimistic. We can achieve much more in our lives when we are in balance, so it is important to generate enthusiasm wherever it is lacking. Enthusiasm differs from person to person, but everyone can recognise when another has it. He or she enjoys and believes in what they do, and their conviction is infectious. Something springs from within them and seems natural. We are magically drawn towards the natural, whether it is a scene in nature, a moment of sincerity between two people, or a person who exudes natural enthusiasm. We are attracted because we know without being told that natural is right.

Unfortunately, we are not so capable of noticing it, or its lack, in ourselves, and furthermore may even have the tendency to sting such positivity in others. We burst the bubble of another when in our opinion their head is too much in the clouds, and they ought to be brought back down to earth. We catch ourselves saying something to our child that was once unthoughtfully said to us, and which we were certain we would never say ourselves. The fact is that the excitement a child feels is natural, as is the nervous anticipation and excitement that a new employee feels when commencing work. Do any of us have the right to dampen that natural enthusiasm? Not at all, but it is done every day in countless families and offices in the name of reality.

Each of us has a responsibility to ourselves to constantly monitor our transformation. Deep down inside each of us rest our inherent scales, which easily tell us when we are out of balance. We have but to listen to them by gauging how we feel at certain times. If every day we wake up and go about our business robotically, without enjoyment, then we are certainly not in balance with what we do. We must ask ourselves if we are following our true vocation, and courageously embrace the answer. If we are not, then our personal transformation will most likely start when we acknowledge the right answer and take action. If we are, then we can examine whether we are allowing distraction to veer us off our true path. When we enjoy vocational balance, we are following our true nature, as we are in tune with what we do, and what we do is an expression of what we are. We are in command of life when we are at one with it.

Unified Diversity

The common theme of ancient wisdom, irrespective of time and culture, has always been to return and follow our original and true nature. The difference between artificiality and naturalness in our lives can be likened to an earnest actor. Using memorised lines and practised gestures, he is able to convince the audience that he is true to the false role he is performing. After the departure of the audience, however, he is able to be himself once more. There is no longer a contradiction between his true self and his acted role. Yet, were he to take the part continuously, a blur between the two identities would result, until the acted, more familiar role, dominated. Although his original nature would always exist, it would remain dormant.

Wherever there exists a well-established artificial nature, disunity within that person is inevitable. With disunity comes tension and strained attempts to control our lives which, paradoxically, actually cause lack of control. To be unified means to be harmoniously at one with ourself. The true natures of two individuals may be as diverse as chalk and cheese, as each individual is unique. But whenever we follow our true nature we are automatically in tune with the natural flow of life.

That is the miracle of life, that in our unified diversity we can each learn to become our own person, fulfilling our own potential and realising our own special meaning and purpose. Yet in following our true nature, we help fulfil the well-intentioned aspirations of those whose paths cross ours, because of our very connectedness with them.

Learning to live with natural spontaneity, acknowledging responsibility in all our personal and interpersonal choices, and seeking balance in how we express ourselves, will unerringly guide us back to our original nature. We have the capability and potential without doubt, but ultimately it is up to each of us, as individuals, to stop blocking our natural path. Transformation from the artificial role into the natural person means doing just that.

> *If you could get rid*
> *Of yourself just once,*
> *The secret of secrets*
> *Would open to you.*
> *The face of the unknown,*
> *Hidden beyond the universe*
> *Would appear on the*
> *Mirror of your perception.*

Rumi

Epilogue

'Three weeks on the road and all that greets me are smouldering ashes,' sighed the Merchant-Sage, Ni.

'What was it that you expected?' said a voice behind him. 'With all the provinces in such chaos! Where have you been?'

Turning round the merchant saw a young man in a bedraggled state, his face stained with blackened smoke and blood. Getting down from his horse, Ni said, 'I had hoped that I would arrive before the Emperor Ch'in's outrages had reached this outpost. But I see that I am too late. Has all been lost?'

'If you are a former graduate of this Academy, as I suspect you are,' said the man, 'you would be wise to take care. For they are imprisoning all who are followers of the ways of the ancients.'

'My ancestor, the renowned Merchant Ni, was the grand-nephew of the founding Patriarch, Wei Tzu. Our House is loyal to the philosophy he and his followers taught. And you—' Ni once more surveyed the man before him, '—what part have you played to be in such a sorry state?'

'I, too, came here for a similar purpose, but alas I was also too late. My name is Lu, of the House of Chou, whose founding father was also a pupil of Wei Tzu. My young heart and legs were sent by my uncle in an attempt to rescue what parchments I could. But all was already aflame when I arrived this morning. It must have burned all night. I have fallen many times and scorched myself in my frantic search, but to no avail.'

The two paused in silence as they surveyed the ruins around them. As they did so, their eyes rested on the head gate stone that now stood *alone, unaccompanied by its former walls. The charred words were still clear to see.*

'So, not all is lost,' said Lu.

'Indeed, none of it can ever be lost,' added Ni, as together they read the stone's inscription.

> *Wisdom comes from one great Sage,*
> *A true source for every age.*
> *Mind, the door, Heart, the key,*
> *Spirit guide, the path to be.*
> *Listen within, Trust to feel,*
> *Illusions vanish, Truth is real.*